Learning Through
Real–World
Problem Solving

D1570768

Learning Through Real-World Problem Solving

The Power of Integrative Teaching

Nancy G. Nagel

CORWIN PRESS, INC.
A Sage Publications Company
Thousand Oaks, California

PHOTO CREDITS: Photos 3.2, 3.3, 3.5, and 3.6 taken by Andy Hebert; Photo 3.16 taken by Annmarie Chesebro; all others taken by Nancy G. Nagel.

For information address:

Corwin Press, Inc.
A Sage Publications Company
2455 Teller Road
Thousand Oaks, California 91320
E-mail: order@corwin.sagepub.com

SAGE Publications Ltd.
6 Bonhill Street
London EC2A 4PU
United Kingdom

SAGE Publications India Pvt. Ltd.
M-32 Market
Greater Kailash I
New Delhi 110 048 India

Printed in the United States of America

Library of Congress Cataloging-in-Publication Data

Nagel, Nancy G.
    Learning through real-world problem solving : The power of integrative teaching / Nancy G. Nagel.
        p. cm.
    Includes bibliographical references and index.
    ISBN 0-8039-6359-9 (cloth: alk. paper).—ISBN 0-8039-6360-2 (pbk.: alk. paper)
    1. Interdisciplinary approach in education—United States.
2. Interdisciplinary approach to knowledge. 3. Elementary school teaching—United States. 4. Active learning. 5. Education, Elementary—United States—Curricula. I. Title.
LB1570.N225   1995
372.19′0973—dc20   95-35442

This book is printed on acid-free paper.

96 97 98 99   10 9 8 7 6 5 4 3 2 1

Corwin Press Production Editor: Tricia K. Bennett

Contents

Foreword

Real Children, Real Problem Solving, Real Learning

Over the past several years, there has been a proliferation of articles and books dealing with the idea of integration in curriculum and teaching. All purport to revise curriculum using some kind of organizing centers other than separate subjects, to devise activities that connect rather than fragment knowledge and to generally increase relevance and liveliness in learning experiences. Worthwhile as those purposes are, their general statement leaves a lot of room for variation. For example, saying that the curriculum will involve organizing centers other than separate subjects, such as themes or topics, does not tell us where those will come from. Will they be chosen by looking for common ground in the existing curriculum, by whatever glossy packaged units are advertised, by teacher interest, or what? And what does making connections across subject areas mean? Will the subjects keep their identities (and time slots) as they contribute to the organizing center, or will they actually be integrated so that knowledge is acquired and used without necessarily naming its disciplinary source?

This may seem like semantic nit-picking, but it is not. The fact is that advocates or reporters of all those variations make basically the same claims about the significance of their curriculum changes as well as the implications for student learning and commitment. Now, if using relevant organizing centers and nonseparate subject activities does have these results, then it stands to reason that the more relevant and the less subject centered the curriculum, the greater the implications for student learning and commitment. In other words, not all curriculum arrangements beyond the separate subject approach are equal. I don't mean to demean those that go a little distance beyond, because they are often big steps for the people and schools involved. But if we want what curriculum integration promises, then we sooner or later search for the most significant organizing centers and the most thorough integration of knowledge.

Note that I did not defend those smaller moves by saying that people have to start somewhere. Yes, we do have to start somewhere, but many people are ready and willing to start a lot farther out than they are given credit for. Take the people involved in this book, for example. We find out well into the book that the teachers who worked with Nancy Nagel on this project—Nalani Wineman, Susan Duncan, Kim Bauer, and Dayle Spitzer—were actually starting from scratch in the kind of work they describe here. Yet the curriculum design they undertake uses real problems as organizing centers, activities that actually integrate knowledge and, in some cases, student participation in decisions about how the curriculum evolved.

By showing their actual unit and lesson plans, they demonstrate that this kind of curriculum is not only possible but that its supposedly ambiguous structure eventually takes on a quite organized quality. This is very important. I have been quite surprised by some of the questions I have been asked about doing curriculum integration, questions that suggest that some teachers are actually unclear about how to do unit teaching, including everything from wondering how knowledge actually gets used to how a calendar of activities gets put together. Probably this should not be surprising because teacher education, like the schools in general, has focused for some time on fragmented, skill-driven, teacher-directed, separate subject methods courses (though the rhetoric of teacher educators would often imply otherwise). So in addition to help in understanding the concepts surrounding problem-centered, integrative teaching, many educators may find some very practical pedagogical information that has generally been lost to obscurity in both preservice and in-service education. Moreover, in the breadth of knowledge integration demonstrated, for those who still wonder what lies beyond the powerful whole language movement, here is a good example.

We will also want to notice that just beneath the surface of this work is one of the most important ideas in the problem-centered, integrative approach, and one that perhaps explains why some people never get this far. The idea is this: Children may be young and they may have certain characteristics of their age, but they live in the world and know what is going on in it. Thus, when we think about what might make for a significant and relevant curriculum for them, we must take into account real problems in our world. In the affectionate rhetoric of developmental appropriateness, too many people seem to think that children are not ready for this kind of work, that the best they can do is teddy bears, apples, and dinosaurs. Thus children are underestimated, and the fact that they live in the real world is ignored. Here, in this book, is evidence that children are aware of problems in the world, can consider how to resolve them, and care about the results.

This is an important book, worth reading for its concepts, its stories, and its celebration of a direction for school curriculum that we should all be thinking about. I hope it is one of many more to come on the problem-centered, integrative approach to curriculum and learning.

James A. Beane
National College of Education,
National-Louis University

Preface

For the past 6 years, I have worked with teachers and students on curriculum development projects focused on integrated or interdisciplinary teaching. This book represents our collective experiences and our beliefs that such teaching within the context of real-world problem solving creates dynamic and meaningful learning experiences for students. Each year, elementary teachers are faced with more content to add to existing curriculum, with little to delete. Today's students need to learn *how* to access and use information. Our knowledge base is expanding at such a rapid rate that traditional curriculum and teaching approaches no longer are effective.

In some elementary schools, there is currently a move to integrate curriculum. There may be a potential problem with the notion of integrated curriculum without a context for this integration. If teachers attempt to integrate curriculum for the purpose of integration alone, perhaps integrated curriculum will become another fad or phase in our education history. Creating a unit around problem solving provides a rich context for integrative teaching and learning as well as providing relevance for students.

The real-world problem-solving units presented in this book were created by four intern teachers, their mentor teachers, and their students. The interns were enrolled in a 14-month teacher education program, the Lewis and Clark College/Oregon Museum of Science and Industry Elementary Intern Program, in Portland, Oregon. This graduate-level program leads to initial teacher licensure and a master's degree. Interns were concurrently involved in a yearlong placement in the schools and education course work. Working in the school setting while developing curriculum enabled interns to receive immediate feedback from their students, mentors, and colleagues about their lessons. Developing and teaching a real-world problem-solving unit is a major emphasis of this teacher education program. It is our intent to share with you the interns' experiences with integrative teaching and learning.

You will read about a group of second graders who examine the front yard of their school and discover a thriving environment that supports a large number of plants, insects, and animals. During their study, they engage in language arts, science, art, mathematics, social studies, use of technology, and public relations (communication arts) as they pursue problems and solutions related to wetlands and land usage. Throughout this book, you will visit classrooms using such a model of integrative teaching and learning. You will watch teachers and students explore thematic topics within a problem-solving approach connected to the real world. Students and teachers work together to identify a problem and share interest and ownership in the emergent curriculum. Examples of units will be presented in a case study format that includes lessons, student work, and feedback about teaching and learning process from students and their teachers.

The primary purpose for writing this book is to provide a resource for educators interested in integrating curriculum, creating relevance in learning, and inviting their students to become involved in shaping the curriculum. Concepts of curriculum are changing from a preconceived, rigid structure to a fluid, emergent format. Students and teachers work together to create the curriculum, activities, and learning as they move through problem solving. Several of the integrative curriculum projects were funded through the Dwight D. Eisenhower Math and Science Education Improvement Program, which provided financial support for workshops and time for teachers to work together to develop curriculum. While teachers explored and developed integrative curriculum based on real-world problem solving, they posed questions such as, "What does this curriculum look like?" "How do we encourage student involvement in the curriculum?" "How do we link classroom learning to life outside of school?" This book is a response to those questions and many others.

The case examples and reflection on experiences of integrative teaching and learning units are directed to understanding and application of real-world problem solving.

Early chapters discuss the rationale and purpose of integrative teaching and learning and lead you to the actual real-world problem-solving units and feedback from students and teachers about their experiences in real-world problem solving. Each unit was taught at a different school, so the contexts represent inner-city schools, suburban schools, and a private school. Later chapters reflect on the implementation of the integrative units and pose recommendations based on these experiences for your teaching.

As you read and explore our ideas and experiences with integrative teaching and learning, we hope you begin to think about your students and how to involve them in real-world problem solving. We found that our students became eager and highly motivated learners as they posed problems, gathered data and researched potential solutions, assumed responsibilities in building curriculum, and reported solutions to the community. We are hopeful that our experiences will entice you into the world of problem solving with your students.

Acknowledgments

To my students, from first graders to graduate students, I have learned from each of you, thank you.

To my colleagues at Lewis and Clark College, Graduate School of Professional Studies; Oregon Museum of Science and Industry; and Amy Driscoll at Portland State University, for your dedication and expertise in improving education and for creating a dynamic, stimulating work environment, thank you.

To Nalani, Susan, Dayle, and Kim, for sharing your stories about teaching and learning, thank you.

To my mother, whose love of the written word was inspirational, thank you.

To my family, Ralph, Marc, and Scott, for your spirit of adventure, with much love, thank you.

Nancy G. Nagel

About the Author

Nancy G. Nagel, Ed.D., is Assistant Professor of Education at Lewis and Clark College in Portland, Oregon. She is coordinator of the Lewis and Clark/Oregon Museum of Science and Industry Elementary Intern Program, which has an emphasis on integrative teaching and learning through real-world problem solving. For the past 6 years, she has been active in integrated curriculum projects, at both the elementary and secondary school levels. Teaching responsibilities include teaching elementary school mathematics and facilitating seminars for mentor teachers and interns. She is also conducting workshops and consulting with school districts about integrated teaching and learning through real-world problem solving. Research interests include studying teaching and learning at the elementary level and the role of gender consciousness in schooling. She is part of a research team studying the changes in schooling that occur when single-sex schools become coeducational and the effect these changes have on students and faculty. Another research interest is exploring how children construct meaning in mathematics. She is currently conducting school-based research on mathematics education with a classroom teacher, with an article describing their emergent collabo rative research process in the fall 1995 issue of *Teacher Researcher*.

About the Contributors

Kim Bauer currently teaches sixth-grade math, science, reading, and design technology at Wy'East Middle School in Hood River, Oregon. She has a B.A. from Pomona College and an M.A.T. from Lewis and Clark College.

Susan Duncan teaches eighth-grade math and science in the Portland Public School District. She earned a B.A. from Macalester College and an M.A.T. from Lewis and Clark College. She continues to develop curriculum using real-world problem-solving projects. She wishes to recognize Cynthia Thomas, Master Teacher, whose guidance made these lessons possible.

Dayle Spitzer earned her M.A.T. at Lewis and Clark College in 1994. She is presently teaching seventh graders on an interdisciplinary team in Hillsboro, Oregon. She continues to work on helping students discover mathematics in their daily lives.

Nalani Wineman facilitates a first- and second-grade blended class at Raleigh Park Elementary School in Beaverton, Oregon. She received her M.A.T. from Lewis and Clark College. Before attending graduate school, she managed biomedical research grants at Scripps Research Institute.

1

Integrative Teaching and Learning Through Real-World Problem Solving

Far from being ends in themselves, the disciplines are means for answering generative "essential" questions. Indeed, armed with the disciplines and with the possibility of interdisciplinary work, individuals are in the best position to revisit these essential questions and to arrive at their own, often deeply personal answers.

—Howard Gardner and
Veronica Boix-Mansilla (1994, p. 17)

Introducing Real-World Problem Solving and Integrative Teaching and Learning

As you know from your own experiences in life, rarely are you confronted with a problem that requires accessing only one discipline to reach a solution. For example, you notice the front tire on your car appears to be flatter than usual, so you make a decision to put more air into the tire. As it has been months since you last filled the tire, you consult the instruction manual that came with your tires. You find you should have 35 pounds per square inch (psi) of air in your tire. Next you drive to the service station and discover you need a quarter to use the air machine. You read the instructions on the machine and, using the tire gauge, check your tire and find you have 25 psi in the tire. You begin to fill your tire, watching the tire and checking the gauge to determine when 35 psi is reached.

While you were immersed in this process you used mathematics to determine the amount of air you needed in the tire, communication skills when you read the manual and the instructions, scientific methods when you made the observation and hypothesis that your tire needed air, and technology to fill the tire to the recommended level. This is an example of a typical problem we might encounter, and although fairly simple to solve, the process required accessing and integrating several disciplines to reach an acceptable solution.

Throughout the book, I prefer to use the phrase *integrative teaching and learning* to emphasize the dynamic process occurring throughout this curriculum and teaching model. Whereas the term *integrated curriculum* implies an emphasis on a fixed, predeveloped curriculum, with integrative teaching and learning, the curriculum or disciplines become integrated, and more important, the teaching and learning process is viewed as changing and dependent on student learning and interests that emerge during the long-term study of a problem. Students are engaged in learning situations that reflect interactive learning in the real world (Shoemaker, 1989).

Integrative teaching and learning through real-world problem solving refers to creating a curriculum drawn from multiple disciplines, various instructional strategies, and learning activities around a selected problem. Why a problem? Problems require a solution, and to reach a solution, the learner becomes actively engaged in a problem-solving process.

As members of society, we play a role in critical decisions that affect our lives and the lives of those in the future. Making an informed decision when voting about the closure of a nearby nuclear plant requires research in several disciplines. We might access scientific knowledge, economics, environmental science, community needs (social studies), and communication skills in our search for information. This process is similar to that used by students working on real-world problem solving. The questions and problems drive the curriculum and learning, and the students lead curriculum development as they search for solutions to problems.

The real-world problems presented in this book revolve around areas of interest to the learners, have relevance to the learners and the larger community, and have no easily apparent solution. The teachers and students selected the problems together and shaped the curriculum as the problem-solving process evolved.

The term *real-world problem solving* is selected to emphasize the importance of creating a meaningful context for learning. Real-world problems are relative to a group of learners and selected through a collaborative process. Within the real-world problem, groups of students may choose to work on specific portions of the problem solving that are of greater interest to them and then come together as a whole group to share ideas and findings. The term *real world* is not meant to delineate learning within and outside of the school. Certainly, we can each think of many real-world problems occurring within a school as easily as we may think of real-world problems outside of a school setting, or problems that might be seen in a smaller version within a school, such as a problem with vandalism or community building. The essence of real-world problem solving is sought through ownership of the problem solving by the students and through the meaning and relevance emerging through studying an area of importance and interest to the learner.

Influences on the Development of Integrated Curriculum

The concept of integrative teaching and learning is definitely not new. John Dewey proposed creating schools around the practice of problem solving through the scientific method, leading to learning through experience in the late 1800s and into the early 1900s. This approach connected school learning with life experiences, similar to the purpose of integrative teaching and learning through real-world problem solving. Dewey (1938) proposed that study "must be derived from materials which at the outset fall within the scope of ordinary life-experience" (p. 73). In Dewey's model of education, life and society outside the school were viewed as relevant, and the curriculum should help students prepare for their future as citizens and workers. Learning by doing was an important component of the education process.

In following Dewey's problem-solving model, student learning would be shaped by problems they encounter. Their involvement in research and activity would teach them a model or process of problem solving that would be applicable in school and in life. Knowledge gained through thinking, research, and experience would lead to learning that is "fused and integrated rather than compartmentalized" (Gutek, 1991, p. 258).

Inquiry-Based Learning

A group of 6- and 7-year-olds noticed that the playground ball always rolled off the playground in the direction of the playing fields. They began talking about the problem of running into games on the playing fields and interrupting the games to collect the playground ball. Why did the ball roll in that direction? The students wanted to find an answer to this question, so they asked their teacher to help them figure out how to check the playground to see if it was higher at one end and if that was why the ball rolled in the direction of the playing fields. Students were seeking new knowledge based on their experiences and their curiosity. The inquiry approach would help them collect and organize their data and learn the skills necessary to obtain an answer to their puzzling question. Ideally, the school would contact the county or other agencies with technical resources for measuring elevation, and students would be involved in the measurement and recording sessions. The information would then lead to several explanations for the ball's rolling, and students could test the explanations to determine the most likely rationale.

A final step might include developing a response or solution to the "ball-rolling problem," such as installing a net near the edge of the playground or even moving the game area to another section of the playground. In inquiry learning students assume responsibility for collecting the information at each step of the inquiry process, with the teacher guiding the students through the inquiry process itself.

During the 1960s and 1970s, many educators became interested in inquiry-based learning or discovery learning. Through this approach, a student's natural curiosity about a subject, topic, or problem drives the student to gather and process information to reach an answer or gain pertinent information. Suchman (1962) believed students could be taught strategies to question and explore events leading to explanations of their new learning. The model is similar to scientific inquiry: beginning with a problem, forming a hypothesis for solving the problem, testing the hypothesis, collecting data, and drawing conclusions.

Joyce, Weil, and Showers (1992) suggest that the inquiry learning environment promotes cooperation, intellectual freedom, and interaction among students. Within the inquiry model, students' interests and needs would shape the curriculum. Often these interests lead to curriculum integration, as students need to access information from many disciplines to reach solutions or explain discrepant events.

Current Interest and Influences
With Integrated Curriculum

Much of the current interest in integrating the school curriculum may be associated with two emerging educational ideas. First, educators are finding themselves increasingly dissatisfied with the distance between school curriculum and life outside the school. Skills learned in school are rarely applicable to problems in the real world (Roth, 1993). Recent reform reports recommend bringing meaning and relevance into the school curriculum. In their publication, *Curriculum and Evaluation Standards for School Mathematics*, The National Council of Teachers of Mathematics (NCTM, 1989) calls for curriculum that is connected to other curricular areas and to the outside world. Integrative teaching and learning through real-world problem solving provides opportunities for interacting with the larger world and becoming part of the solution, while providing a resource and service to the community.

In my experiences with young students, I often hear the question, "What does this have to do with me?" Students are trying to connect with curriculum that seems to lack relevance. By exploring problem solving and having a role in shaping the direction of the curriculum, students find meaning as they search for answers and solutions to their questions in integrative teaching and learning.

A second major influence on the development of current curriculum and instructional strategies is found in the growing interest in constructivism as a learning model. According to von Glaserfeld (1987), within the constructivist model, we come to see knowledge and competence are "products of the individual's conceptual organization of the individual's experience" (p. 16). He further states that "the teacher's role will no longer be to dispense 'truth' but rather to help and guide the student in the conceptual organization of certain areas of experience" (p. 16). With this approach to teaching and learning, we would find the teacher assisting students throughout the learning process, providing examples, activities, and experiences that help students acquire knowledge, organize this knowledge, and make connections between the new knowledge and prior learning to create personal meaning. For example, several students noticed the moon in the sky as they walked to school in the early morning. They entered the classroom discussing what they had seen and wondering about the different phases of the moon. The teacher listened to their conversation and watched them as they began to draw the moon phases and attempt to label each phase. She joined their conversation and asked where they might find more information about moons and also where they might experience moon phases. The students started talking about an older sister's science class and decided to talk to her and look at her books and materials. One student suggested keeping a night journal and drawing the moon for a month. Soon these ideas became a "plan" and the students were moving forward in their acquisition of knowledge, searching for answers and meaning to make sense of their beginning knowledge of lunar phases. Throughout the learning process the teacher assisted the students in accessing more information as she listened to them and asked questions that allowed them to continue their quest for knowledge.

The constructivist view of education supports an environment where students engage in authentic learning with opportunity to explore and expand their knowledge. Noddings (1990) writes, "The constructivist position . . . recognizes the power of the environment to press for adaptation, the temporality of knowledge, and the existence of multiple selves behaving in consonance with the rules of various subcultures" (p. 12). This message reminds educators that schools can be places where teachers and students share in constructing meaning as they gain knowledge in their search for understanding.

In a constructivist classroom, the focus is on the learner, with the teacher inviting "students to experience the world's richness, empower them to ask their own questions and seek their own answers, and challenge them to understand the world's complexities" (Brooks & Brooks, 1993, p. 5). Certainly this view of teaching and learning supports the process of integrative teaching and learning through problem solving, with students building their curriculum as they ask questions and seek answers or solutions to problems they are pursuing.

The concept of integrative teaching and learning is grounded in constructivism, as students are actively involved in relevant problem solving and accessing knowledge from multiple disciplines. Students make their own sense of the problem and of the process as they move through problem solving. Meaning is created by the students in the integrative curriculum driven by real-world problem solving, allowing students to "use their knowledge and skills to search for answers to their questions rather than to concentrate on passing exams" (Beane, 1992, p. 3). Generally, there is not one answer for the problem, so students are engaged in an open-ended situation as they construct meaning across multiple disciplines. In both the constructivist model and integrative teaching and learning, learning is viewed as an activity pursued by the student, with learners engaged in their environment and as active participants in constructing knowledge (Pace, 1992), which is in sharp contrast to the belief that knowledge is simply transmitted from a teacher to students.

Models of Integrated Curriculum

Integration of One Curricular Discipline Into Other Disciplines

In the mid-1970s, writing across the curriculum was introduced to elementary and secondary schools throughout the country. Educators participated in workshops and classes promoting the integration of writing into classes other than language arts. Teachers and students began exploring writing in social studies, science, mathematics, and additional subject areas. For many teachers of subjects other than language arts, this was the first time they had considered integrating writing as part of their teaching, and they soon recognized that writing in the content area led to increased learning. Teachers began "teaching writing as practiced in all disciplines by teaching it through all the school subjects" (Moffett, 1992a, p. 11). Educators noted learning gains when students were actively involved in writing within different subject areas, and writing across the curriculum was accepted as a viable model in many school districts.

Fulwiler (1987) recommends that "more teachers in all disciplines need to study the several dimensions of language which most actively promote clear writing and critical reasoning" (p. 11) as we help students develop writing and thinking skills across the curriculum. Many teachers are involved in professional development, through their improvement of personal writing skills, as they learn how to improve the teaching of their content area with writing as an important learning component. Students benefit from the focus on writing across the curriculum, because they improve their writing and thinking through assignments and assessments that encourage them to express themselves through writing. The act of writing helps us think about the subject or topic we are exploring and connect new thoughts and prior learning. For instance, when 8-year-olds are writing about the similarities and differences between being an 8-year-old in the neighborhood and an 8-year-old in Costa Rica, they think about their own activities and surroundings and compare and contrast this to their knowledge of life in Costa Rica. While they are immersed in their writing and research, they are also analyzing, synthesizing, and assessing the similarities and differences, all leading to critical thinking. The writing process then becomes an avenue for expanding thinking and learning and moves beyond the type of learning that might occur from a lecture or reading from a textbook, because the child now becomes personally engaged in the learning.

Other attempts of integrating one discipline into other disciplines are found in teaching reading within a specific content area, science and math integration, and integration of computer technology into a content area. These approaches are typically concerned with integrating one content area into another content area or teaching two related disciplines simultaneously. Often the differences between the disciplines are highlighted, with distinct disciplinary boundaries noted.

Whole Language Approach

The whole language model promotes learning reading and writing in a meaningful context, "allowing children more choices, writing for authentic purposes, considering holistic strategies for at-risk students, establishing a collaborative classroom, evaluating, questioning our teaching" (Routman, 1991, p. 3) in creating a successful learning environment. Students continue to learn to read and write from the language foundation they bring to school. Teachers are committed to a meaningful approach to learning and to enabling students to guide their own learning. Watson (1989) defines whole language as a "perspective on education that is supported by beliefs about learners and learning, teachers and teaching, language, and curriculum" (p. 133). The teacher focuses on the strengths of each student and becomes a facilitator and colearner throughout the learning process. Language, reading, and writing are truly integrated in the whole language approach to teaching and learning, with the teacher and students collaborating together to improve their literacy. Presently, the whole language model is being implemented in more classrooms and is impacting the learning of language arts along with the overall classroom learning environment.

Middle School Movement

During the 1970s and 1980s, many schools for young adolescents moved from the junior high school model, basically a preparation for high school as the name denotes, to a middle school model. Alexander and McEwin (1989) reported that from 1970-1971 to 1986-1987 the number of schools with a configuration composed of grades 6 through 8 increased from 1,663 to 4,329, representing an increase of 160%. During the same period, the number of schools with a grade 7 to grade 9 configuration decreased by 53%.

Grade configuration is certainly not as important as the school program in determining whether the school is organized as a mini high school or as a middle-level program. Grade levels of middle schools vary but represent some configuration drawn from grades 5 through 9. Middle schools operate with the belief that education for these students (typically, the 10- to 15-year-old) is sensitive to this age group's specific learning needs and stages of adolescent development. Characteristics of most middle school programs include interdisciplinary teaming, block scheduling, teacher advisory or home room sessions, and cocurricular activities (Valentine, Clark, Irvin, Keefe, & Melton, 1993). Many middle schools have implemented an extended block of time in the school schedule, ranging from two to five periods, with teachers working together with the same group of students. The team of teachers also has shared planning times. This approach to teaming enables teachers from different disciplines to coordinate themes within their subject area and to share perspectives of the same group of students. Both teachers and students benefit from the interdisciplinary teaming as they share common learning experiences, creating a sense of community within the school (Carnegie Council, 1989).

In some middle schools, teachers integrate the curriculum, but in others the shared blocks of time primarily exist to allow teachers to share information about students. Interdisciplinary teaching encompasses a range of teaching possibilities, with the shared group of students as the common link. Often, teachers are responsible for a specific subject area and curriculum content and find that integrating the curriculum may work for specific units, yet integrated curriculum tends to be an occasional occurrence during the school year. Under the term *interdisciplinary teaming*, the range of practice may include shared blocks of teaching time with the same students, with no curriculum integration or common planning, to full interdisciplinary teaching, with all teachers working together to plan and present integrated curriculum during the daily extended block period.

Team Teaching

Another model of team teaching that may lead to integrated curriculum is found when several teachers of the same or various grade levels, at the elementary school, work as a team in developing curriculum. For example, a fifth-grade team of teachers may decide to teach a unit on Canada. One teacher is responsible for teaching about the history of Canada, another teacher presents information about current life in Canada, and the third teacher uses the Internet to allow students to carry on a conversation with a group of fifth graders in British Columbia. The teachers rotate through the three classrooms and teach one group of students at a time. In this model, teaming is seen as a way to share curriculum assignments and allow teachers to specialize in one area of the curriculum unit. In some instances the team teaching involves integrating the curriculum, although not in every situation.

Mathematics and Science Education Emphasis on Problem Solving

National standards in mathematics (NCTM, 1989) are calling for problem solving to be a major focus of mathematics education, with problems representing real-life scenarios. The American Association for the Advancement of Science (AAAS, 1989) also emphasizes the importance of engaging students in problem solving and activities that reflect meaningful experiences. When examining problem solving as a relevant activity and connected to real life, the integration of curriculum and of teaching and learning becomes apparent. In looking back at the example of the tire needing air and the access of multiple disciplines to solve the problem, the importance of integrative teaching and learning is reinforced.

Other Integrated Curriculum Models

Robin Fogarty (1991) presents 10 models for integrating and connecting the curriculum, spanning a broad continuum. These models include the following:

fragmented (separate and distinct disciplines)

connected (course content is connected topic to topic)

nested (targeting multiple skills)

sequenced (topics within each discipline are arranged to be taught at the same time)

shared (sharing planning and teaching in two disciplines)

webbed (using a theme to sift our concepts and topics)

threaded (threading a specific skill or focus through the disciplines)

integrated (match subjects for overlaps in topics and concepts)

immersed (learner becomes immersed in the experience)

networked (learner filters learning through the expert and makes internal connections)

Her work provides an overview of different strategies and models of curriculum integration, with information for applying these models into the classroom. Many of these models fit simultaneously within the real-world problem-solving model as students search for solutions as they access multiple disciplines and experts when immersed in problem solving.

Real-World Problem-Solving Model

In the real-world problem-solving model presented in this book, students work in meaningful situations as they examine the problem, gather data, research relevant information and resources, contact experts in the field for current findings, work collaboratively to divide and share tasks, and test possible solutions. As a culminating activity, the solution (or in some cases, the reframing of the problem) is presented to the larger community and to agencies or organizations dealing with the problem. Students access knowledge and information from multiple disciplines as needed. There are no arbitrary lines delineating one discipline from another. The teacher's role becomes one of resource specialist, assisting students to locate information through computer networks; local, state, and national agencies; libraries; and other sources appropriate to the problem.

In later chapters, several examples of real-world problems and the integrative teaching and learning created around solving the problems will be explored. The teachers and students provide insights into the integrative approach to learning. In each classroom, teachers and students spent time exploring the problem in the initial phase of the unit. The problem-solving process shaped the unit, resulting in building an emergent curriculum and leading to student-centered learning. In one classroom, the students became so involved with exploring the role of salmon in the life of Native Americans that the unit continued to examine the impact of salmon on numerous groups of people, including those living in the present time.

When selecting a real-world problem, students discussed problems or concerns of interest to them. Problems were to be of interest to the community as well, so students identified local issues and developed lists of problems needing attention in their community. Many of the problems from these groups of students dealt with environmental issues, possibly with the influence of the Northwest culture and its concern over logging issues, salmon extinction, water pollution, and misuse of natural resources. Students were excited to explore areas they had heard about on the news or seen in the newspaper. It became a difficult task to narrow the list to the final choice of one problem.

Integrative Teaching and Learning: A Place Within the Curriculum

The curriculum in the elementary school seems to be ever expanding. New topics are added each year, increasing the amount of material to be learned and leading to fragmentation of learning.

Outcome-based education looks at meeting certain goals on an established time schedule. So how does a teacher add integrative teaching and learning to the school day? The operative word in this question is add, as integrative teaching and learning may not add much to the curriculum as it changes the traditional configuration of the separate presentation of disciplines. Problem solving provides a context for the basic skills pertinent to a distinct discipline and an avenue to use when exploring and searching for answers to problems. Educators are encouraged to consider the "quality of understanding over quantity of coverage" (Rutherford & Ahlgren, 1990, p. 185) and that "less is more" (Sizer, 1986, p. 40).

Through an integrative teaching and learning approach, students build on the basic skills taught in the early years of schooling. The problem-solving process allows them to actually use these basic skills in science, mathematics, language arts, social studies, and fine arts in a dynamic, interesting format. It is essential to understand that integrative teaching and learning does not replace discipline-based knowledge. Students continue to learn basic skills and knowledge and then "practice" and expand this knowledge base as they explore problem solving. The integrative approach "does not ask whether there should be subject matter or skills but rather how those are brought into the lives of young people and used by them" (Beane, 1993, p. 19). When involved in meaningful learning, students have the opportunity to expand and connect discipline knowledge and skills within the context of relevant problem solving.

Students are also engaged in critical thinking and decision making with integrative teaching and learning, which is an essential goal of our education programs. This thinking and decision making occur around problem solving and communicating findings to a larger community, allowing for application of basic skills within the meaningful context of a community issue or problem.

In some classrooms, the real-world problem-solving unit might be part of the school day on a daily basis of 30 to 40 minutes over the entire school year. In other classes, students might work on the problem two to three times a week for longer time blocks. In another room, it might work best to spend a half day per week (perhaps when the class has access to computers) on the problem-solving process. Each teaching setting will be different, with time allocated to the problem solving determined by many events, demands, and priorities. The main decision is to make integrative teaching and learning a core of the curriculum and establish a time frame that supports the selected problem, student's needs, and learning activities. In the examples presented in later chapters, each classroom worked with a different timeline for the problem-solving process, and a discussion of strengths and suggestions for designing time periods will follow each example.

Summary

Looking at integrative teaching and learning and the influences leading to integrated curriculum makes one wonder if this is another fad or phase in education. A closer look at the importance of creating meaningful contexts for students in our classrooms spurs us on to explore the potential of integrative teaching and learning. A variety of models of integrating curriculum have evolved over the years and have met with success. The pull to creating relevance and connections to life demands scrutinizing the existing school curriculum. Implementation of integrative teaching and learning through real-world problem solving enables students to gain and apply knowledge from many disciplines as they construct meaning and make sense of their world.

2

Why Implement an Integrative Teaching and Learning Model?

We need to assure an empowering education for everyone attending our schools. Our students need to be able to use knowledge, not just know about things. Understanding is about making connections among and between things, about deep and not surface knowledge, and about greater complexity, not simplicity.

—Vito Perrone (1994, p. 13)

Learning in Context

Your community is exploring the issue of whether a major corporation should be given permission to build a golf course in the local area. You are personally committed to making an informed decision about this development and the impact the golf course would have on your community. To educate yourself, you research the effects the golf course would have in the areas of economics, environment, and quality of life on the community. To become well informed, you access knowledge from social sciences, science, mathematics, communication arts, and aesthetics. As you gain knowledge, you are not concerned with boundaries between disciplines, rather you are gathering knowledge within the context of the problem you are attempting to solve.

And so it is with integrative teaching and learning. Students and the teacher work together to solve problems within the context of the problem. Students draw meaning from the *whole*, rather than from fragmented pieces of disciplines. As you learned about the impact of the golf course on your community, your knowledge would be limited if you looked only at the financial impact. You would not have the total or whole picture. When the problem itself provides a context for learning, learning takes on meaning. Gaining knowledge through the disciplines allows you to become informed and make sense of the problem.

When involved in the integrative teaching and learning model, students work in small groups to research portions of the problem, reporting to the whole class on a regular basis, because one group's findings might affect the direction of the research in another group. In the golf course example, one group might conduct a poll of community members about use of and interest in recreational opportunities. Another group might talk to local environmental agencies while yet another group charts wildlife populations residing in the area near the proposed golf course site. Students draw on prior knowledge in all areas to share and collaborate on the problem solving. There are no artificial boundaries separating disciplines. Working together on the problem solving, students use mathematics (e.g., counting and predicting number of species living in region), communication (e.g., conducting a survey with local residents), social studies (e.g., researching prior use of area), science (e.g., determining and monitoring changes in water quality), and art (e.g., drawing or painting scenes to represent past use of area, current use of area, and predicted use of area). Students are involved in creating new knowledge within the context of the problem and without concern for discipline boundaries.

Relevance in Learning

One of the more frequently heard complaints from students is criticism related to not understanding "why we have to learn this." Students become memorizers of information that will be required on a test and often decide school is a place where you figure out what the teacher wants you to know. Much of the traditional school curriculum is viewed as required learning without a sense of connection to the world outside of school. This view of schooling is in sharp contrast to the view presented by Dewey, as discussed in Chapter 1. Dewey (1938) encourages the engagement of learners in experiences that are relevant to life and supports the development of citizens who have the ability to think beyond the memorization of facts. In a democratic society, we rely on all citizens to be informed and make sound decisions that affect our lives in many ways.

When observing young children at play, we find purpose in their activities as they create meaning and relevance with questions and explorations. They often direct their learning to find out why or how something works as it does. As children go through their elementary years, they come to realize that large portions of school are separate from the rest of their world. In later elementary grades, students search for relevance and meaning in their school work. Integrative teaching and learning through real-world problem solving responds to this need. The integrative teaching and learning model is grounded in connections between disciplines and connecting school with life in the community. Through the problem-solving approach, students set goals, purpose, and directions for their learning and work together to gather information and share knowledge, both within their class and with the community. Relevance and importance of learning are apparent to the learner, parents, educators, and the community.

Information and Knowledge Explosion

The 21st century is around the corner. New information and knowledge increase daily at a rapid rate. New careers will be developed in the next decade that are far different from current employment patterns. Training and education for these careers are nonexistent, because the careers are yet to be defined. Many of you might have found yourselves to be proficient with a specific computer or software program and then find that the hardware or software has been upgraded and you must learn how to use the new programs or equipment to continue your work. Computers, communication fields (e.g., E-mail), and multimedia technology are a few of the many areas that are changing at a rapid pace. How are students in school today to be prepared to meet requirements for careers as yet to be created? How does the school curriculum respond to the explosion of information?

It is no longer possible or preferable to memorize knowledge to become an educated person. In a review of futurists' views of education in the coming years, Benjamin (1989) advocated a shift from the "passive acquisition of discipline-based subject matter to one of . . . active seeking of knowledge by each student" (p. 11). Students will use knowledge and learn how to access critical information to become prepared for future employment and the responsibilities of citizenship.

Integrative teaching and learning through problem solving provides a learning model in which students become involved in a community issue and assume a contributing role, through gathering data and knowledge from many resources, to aid in decision making or further clarification of issues related to the problem. As students proceed through the problem-solving process, they access current information by calling experts on the telephone, writing letters to interested parties, gathering data through various computer networks, conversing with experts on a worldwide basis through electronic mail, and providing their own findings as new information. This process enables students to learn about the importance of current findings and status and how to access up-to-date information. Textbooks may provide historical background information and additional points of view, but they are viewed as only a small part of the resource pool, with a need to pay attention to accessing current and recent information to complete a well-rounded study. Students access information through technology as they create new learning from their prior knowledge and synthesis of current data. Involvement in integrative teaching and learning teaches students a learning model applicable to the exploding information age in which they live.

Teaching for Understanding

Sixty teachers in the Boston area collaborated with researchers from the Harvard Graduate School of Education in designing educational practices to support teaching for understanding. The participants in the Teaching for Understanding Project investigated the nature of understanding, developed ways to teach and assess for understanding, and analyzed teaching for understanding practices implemented within the framework developed through the project (Perkins & Blythe, 1994). Teaching for understanding became an educational priority when educators recognized that students were not understanding key concepts in mathematics, sciences, history, or literature. In an interview conducted by Siegel and Shaughnessy (1994), Howard Gardner raises concern about the status of American education, with students "just going through the motions of education" (p. 563). In contrast, teaching for understanding moves the level of learning to one where students "take knowledge, skills, and other apparent attainments and apply them successfully in new situations" (p. 564). Students who understand the topic or concept are able to demonstrate this knowledge through a "variety of performances that display understanding and advance the topic" (Perkins & Blythe, 1994, p. 6).

Perkins (1992) points out that our goals in education should reflect " 'generative knowledge'—knowledge that does not just sit there but functions richly in people's lives to help them understand and deal with the world" (p. 5). To reach this level of learning, students must be able to retain knowledge, understand knowledge, and actively use knowledge (Perkins, 1992). In addition, Perkins recommends that schools focus on thoughtful learning, in which students are engaged and learn through active involvement in meaningful thinking. We find students involved in problem solving to be immersed in thoughtful inquiry as they conduct research, ask questions, contact experts, and bring their information together to examine solutions to problems. All of these activities reflect the goals of "generative knowledge," as portrayed by Perkins.

In integrative teaching and learning through real-world problem solving, students actively engage in seeking understanding and new meaning around a problem or issue. Students conduct research, consult experts, contact community members, and share findings as they explore solutions for the problem. They develop charts, graphs, timetables, documents, videos, and other relevant materials to display their findings. The culminating event for most problem-solving units will be the presentation of findings and a potential solution to the problem to the larger community of concerned citizens. Students pose possible solutions and examine effects each solution may have on the community. The final presentation is a demonstration of students' understanding of the problem or issue and of their understanding and interpretation of findings (advancement of knowledge) derived from in-depth research.

Acknowledging Multiple Intelligences

Howard Gardner has presented educators with a model for thinking about intelligence and about teaching that reflects the importance of accessing these seven intelligences. The seven intelligences (linguistic, logical-mathematical, spatial, musical, bodily-kinesthetic, interpersonal, and intrapersonal) "work together to solve problems, to yield various kinds of cultural endstates—vocations, avocations, and the like" (Gardner, 1993, p. 9). Gardner supports the notion that the purpose of schools should be to further develop these intelligences. To accomplish this goal, schools move toward a student-centered orientation, allowing students to pursue their interests in an environment that recognizes that students learn differently and that they should have choices in their curriculum and learning experiences.

Certainly, we see a close connection between teaching with attention to multiple intelligences and integrative teaching and learning through problem solving, with students engaged in a rich variety of activities, pursuing individual interests and questions to gain new knowledge. Providing resources and activities in the school that acknowledge the seven intelligences would also support problem solving. For instance, students working on a problem of water availability might choose to work with the music specialist and compose a song to share their research, using musical, linguistic, and, possibly, bodily-kinesthetic intelligence, if they choose to move or dance to their music. Many of the resources that support learning in each of the seven intelligences are available within the school or the community. The teacher's role again becomes one of resource specialist, with an understanding and appreciation for including experiences in multiple intelligences as resources and opportunities are brought to the classroom.

Contributing to the Larger Community

By identifying a problem or issue of importance to the community, students moved the locus of their learning beyond the school classroom to the real world or the community outside of school. In this era, the public is bombarded with rhetoric about losing community. In past decades, generations of families resided in the same neighborhood, town, or vicinity. As employment patterns changed, so did the sense of connectedness to one community. Families moved to different states and corners of the country. The makeup of families also changed. Grandparents and other relatives who are part of the extended family are often not living near each other, and the nuclear family has many configurations beyond the traditional mother, father, and children.

Clearly, the support from and connection to community is now different. Children need help to bridge the world of school to the larger community in which they live. Through real-world problem solving, students become engaged in an issue of importance to themselves and to their community. The research and knowledge the students gain is applicable to a real issue, and the findings become important to the community. In the best sense, students find themselves contributing to solving a problem or issue and helping to improve their own community. Toffler (1981) and Shuman (1984) recommend that schools consider learning with a focus on real problems as a format that allows students to provide services to the community. The learning gained by the students is not artificial or learned merely to pass the chapter exam but is meaningful and useful to a larger audience. Through real-world problem solving, students become contributing members of the community and make connections with their work and the outside world.

Summary

Implementing an integrative teaching and learning model through real-world problem solving provides a rich, meaningful context for learning and a holistic approach to curriculum. Fragmentation and division between disciplines is decreased as students explore and create knowledge through problem solving. Students use their prior knowledge and create new knowledge as they research the problem and gather data. Connections between purpose for knowledge and actual use of the knowledge are apparent as students apply and synthesize new learning.

While researching the problem and testing possible solutions, students find the learning to be relevant and to have a purpose. Decisions are guided by findings and shared with classmates to create a whole picture of the problem, issues, and potential impact of the solution. Students collaborate to make meaning of their work while aware of the purpose for their research and results.

Real-world problem solving teaches students how to access information in this rapidly expanding information age. Moving beyond the textbook teaches students to identify and use appropriate sources that provide current and accurate information.

A frequent complaint about today's education is the lack of understanding exhibited by students. The public is concerned about a perceived decline in the knowledge base of students. Teaching for understanding requires students to use knowledge and demonstrate use of the knowledge in a variety of formats. When working in real-world problem solving, students use knowledge to reach solutions and demonstrate their understanding of learning as they present findings and share research with others.

Selecting a real-world problem provides an opportunity for students to make important contributions to their own community. Developing and presenting solutions to problems or issues to concerned citizens allows students to practice becoming informed and active community members. Real-world problem solving provides a rich context with deep meaning for students as they search for solutions to problems and issues of concern to themselves and to the community.

3

Looking in the Classrooms

CASE STUDIES INTRODUCTION

Imagine a group of 10- and 11-year-old children who are so interested in the many controversial issues surrounding the possible extinction of salmon that they decide to compose a newspaper to reach special interest groups, legislators, educators, and agencies that influence decision making concerning issues about salmon. You will visit this group of students in this chapter and learn how other students and teachers might use problem solving as a fertile learning ground that produces meaningful results.

In this chapter, four case studies of integrative teaching and learning units developed around real-world problems are presented and described. Each of these units was developed by an intern teacher enrolled in the Elementary Intern Program at Lewis and Clark College in Portland, Oregon. Interns were completing course work over a 14-month period leading to a master's degree and initial teaching licensure. Each intern worked with a mentor teacher during a year-long school placement, concurrent with education course work and seminars held on campus. A major emphasis of this teacher education program is the development and teaching of a real-world problem-solving unit. Interns developed the unit with support from several sources, including a course titled Thematic Inquiry, taught by Rosemary

Wray Williams. This course brought together concepts of real-world problem solving, curriculum development, and integrative teaching and learning. In addition, mentor teachers attended seminars focused on real-world problem-solving units and worked with their interns in developing the units. Intern seminars also concentrated on the theory and application of real-world problem solving. Drawing from this knowledge base and with support from mentors and college faculty, interns worked with their students to create and teach dynamic units representing integrative teaching and learning.

This chapter highlights the results of four interns' work with real-world problem solving. Your visit to each classroom will include an overview of the unit, a series of 8 to 12 lesson plans, a material list for each lesson, and applicable resources. Each unit was taught at a different school, and the school setting and population will be discussed to provide a context or background for the teaching and learning of the unit. The units are easily transferable or adaptable to different schools and grade levels. The reader might be interested in the reasons teachers and students selected specific problems and how learning activities were organized to match the problem-solving process. The selection process of the real-world problems and the ways that student learning and interests shaped future lessons will be discussed in depth in Chapters 5 and 6.

Although the reader will see finished versions of real-world problem-solving units, it is important to remember that much of the unit was shaped as the learning evolved. The unit overview and lessons were planned with the understanding that lessons would change direction once students began their research and selected various areas to investigate based on the problem-solving process itself. The teachers included background information and knowledge in the early lessons and moved toward a model of the students selecting topics to research and investigate after they gained an understanding of the larger problem. In each of these classrooms, students created a final project, demonstrating their growth in problem solving and extensive research in an area or part of the problem that was deemed interesting and important by the student or small group of students involved in developing the final project.

The lesson plans presented in this section were rewritten by the intern teachers after their students completed the problem-solving process and with the specific purpose of sharing with you, the reader. Each group of students will guide their own understanding of a problem and their unique problem-solving process. The units presented here represent examples of problem-solving units that might be of interest to other students and may help teachers formulate problems and units with their students.

Integrative teaching and learning is highlighted throughout the units. As the lessons unfold and students engage in problem solving, the lines between disciplines dissolve. Students explore new areas of knowledge with the purpose of seeking information relevant to problem solving and construct new meaning based on their prior knowledge and the research conducted to create solutions. Again, we find that students' work with real-world problem solving provides the context for integrating the curriculum.

SEXTON MOUNTAIN ELEMENTARY SCHOOL AND WETLANDS

Students at Sexton Mountain Elementary School in Beaverton, Oregon, attend school in a unique setting. At the front entrance to the school is a preserved wetlands area, with plants and wildlife protected from development. Nalani Wineman, the intern teacher whose work is presented in this section of the book, took advantage of this extraordinary opportunity and worked with her students to develop a real-world problem related to the wetlands area. Students became involved in exploring the wetland, gathering information about the land, making decisions about land use, and presenting their findings to the community.

Sexton Mountain Elementary School is in the Beaverton School District, located approximately 20 miles west of Portland, Oregon. The school area is now surrounded by numerous housing developments that have been under continual construction since the 1980s. Prior to the development, the school grounds were used as farmland. The school's development was completed during the summer of 1989; it is situated on low, sloping meadowland. The building is quite modern, with open classroom areas surrounding the media center. There are also five portable classroom buildings, erected to meet the growing enrollment needs. The student body consists of 790 students in kindergarten through Grade 6, with 74 teachers, administrators, and support staff employed at the school.

Approximately 86% of the students are Caucasian, 11% Asian/ Pacific Islanders, 2% Hispanic, and 1% African American. The majority

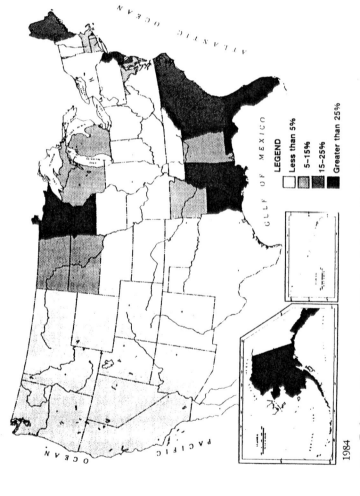

Figure 3.1. Relative Abundance of Wetlands in the United States
SOURCE: Tiner (1984). Reprinted with permission by the U.S. Fish and Wildlife Services.

of the students are considered middle class, with few children receiving either free or reduced-price lunches. Parent support of the school is evident through volunteer work provided at the school and the number of special events and fund-raising activities sponsored to benefit the students. Parents also help in the media center, classrooms, computer labs, and science labs. The school has many computers and on-line programs that are accessed on a continual basis by the students and faculty. Sexton Mountain Elementary School is a rich learning environment with teachers and parents committed to a quality education for students.

The integrative teaching and learning presented in the following section was taught to a group of second-grade students over a 12-week period. Prior to this unit, students had completed a unit about endangered species, which provided a natural lead into the wetland unit.

Our Front Yard:
Choices in Land Development

Unit Overview. There is a possibility that the land in front of Sexton Mountain Elementary School might be landscaped in the near future. Second graders will be exploring the front yard of the school and gathering essential information to make decisions about landscaping. Included in a portion of the front yard of the school is a wetlands area, with specific planning use guidelines developed by the federal, state, and county governments. These guidelines will provide additional direction to the students and be incorporated in their planning and decision making.

Unit Goals. Students will work through problem-solving processes to explore the importance of wetland areas; gather critical information for land use decisions; analyze impact of land development on wildlife, plants, people, and the community; and present findings to community members.

Unit Activities
1. Explore the front yard of the school and identify plants and animals that live in this area of land.

2. Develop a map of their own front yard, noting objects and plants in their yard.

3. Measure the front yard of the school, finding the perimeter and square footage of the area.

4. Make several checks on elevation of different areas of the school's front yard.

5. Identify the school grounds in an aerial photograph, comparing and contrasting the change in land usage over a period of 20 years as noted in the aerial photographs.

6. Draw pictures of the various animals and insects living in the wetlands area in the front yard of the school.

7. Write stories about the animals (creatures) and their habitats in the front yard of the school.

8. Identify several natural wetland plants and explain one function of a plant that is found in the front yard of the school.

9. Discover several qualities of wetland soil.

10. Create and use metaphors to discuss the basic conditions and processes occurring in a wetland.

11. Plan a video presentation about the students' work with the front yard of the school.

12. Compare and contrast students' knowledge of and thoughts about landscaping and/or use of the front yard of the school from before the unit to their knowledge at the end of the unit.

Note: Nalani (the teacher of this unit) purposely avoided using the term *wetland* in the first lessons. She wanted the students to come to their own stance about the use of the land based on their research and investigations.

Lesson #1: What Is in Our Front Yard?

Objective. Visit the front yard of the school and observe the plants, animals, and other objects found in this area.

Opening Activity. Each student draws a picture of the front yard of the school, adding as much detail as possible from memory.

Photo 3.1. Wetlands Area in Front of Sexton Mountain
Elementary School

Lesson Activities
1. Students walk to the front yard of the school and explore the entire area, placing small flags in the ground to define the perimeter of this area.
2. Students discuss and share their findings with their partners as they walk around the designated area.
3. Returning to the classroom, students brainstorm everything they observed in the designated area. Student comments and questions will be recorded on a large sheet of butcher paper.

Closing Activity. Students discuss these questions: "What makes up our front yard?" and "Is it waiting to be landscaped?" in their journals. Journal entries may be shared with small groups.

Materials
1. Paper for drawing picture of front yard
2. Small plastic flags on wire posts
3. Butcher paper and pens
4. Journals

Lesson #2: Posing the Problem of Landscaping the School Yard

Objective. Students compare and contrast the front yard of their school to other schools' yards.

Opening Activity. Students read aloud from the list of "the content of the front yard" that was created following their visit to the front yard in the previous lesson.

Lesson Activities
1. Students view a video clip showing the front yards of four different schools.
2. Students compare these front yards to the front yard of their own school and list similarities and differences.
3. Students respond to these questions: "What should be done with our front yard?" and "Who should we share our ideas with?"
4. Research categories (areas to explore to find answers to the problem of what and how to landscape the area) will be generated from the list of ideas about what should be done with our front yard. Categories might include history of area, land, vegetation, creatures, and the like.

Closing Activity. Students select two research categories they are most interested in exploring and write an explanation of their interest in their journal.

Materials
1. Video depicting four different school front yards
2. VCR
3. Butcher paper and pens
4. Journals

Lesson #3: Land Topography

Objective. Students discuss elevation changes as noticed when in the school's front yard and describe the elevation changes, using the contour map of the area.

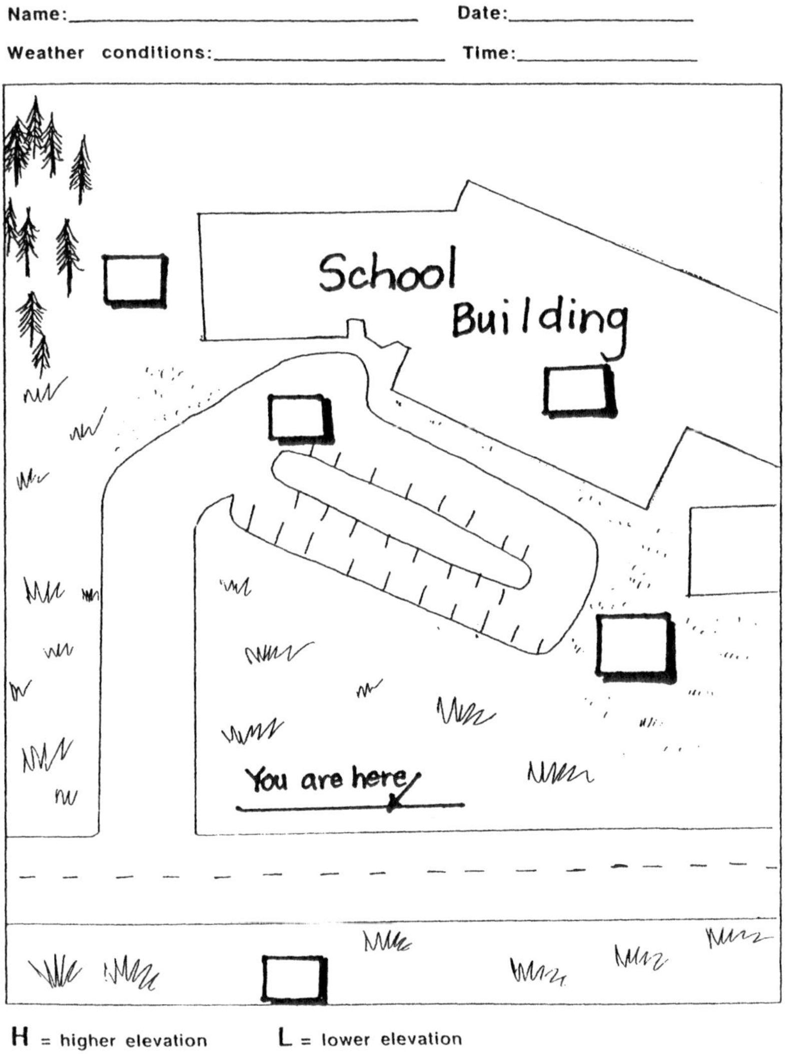

Name:_____   Date:_____

Weather conditions:_____   Time:_____

H = higher elevation   L = lower elevation

Figure 3.2. Estimated Elevation
NOTE: Drawn by Nalani Wineman.

Opening Activity. Discuss up and down, higher and lower, and the meaning of elevation. Has anyone been in an elevator? Where do you go?

Lesson Activities

1. Using the overhead projector, look at a simple map of the front yard of the school. On the map (Figure 3.2), note the four empty boxes, which are the places to record H for high spot and L for low spot.

2. Each child has a map of the front yard on a clipboard, with a pencil attached. The students are now researchers and explore the elevation of the front yard.

3. Students take turns standing in each of the four spots marked on the map. Plastic flags highlight these spots outside. Students now determine if each of the four spots is a low spot or a high spot, marking their response (H or L) on the map.

Closing Activity. On returning to the classroom, students observe a three-dimensional contour map and note the elevation lines drawn to represent elevation. Students then draw elevation lines on their own maps around one low area and one high area.

Materials

1. Overhead projector
2. Simple map of front yard
3. Clipboard with pencil for each student
4. Four plastic flags
5. Three-dimensional contour map

Lesson #4: History of Front Yard Land Use and Soil Types

Objective. Students identify school grounds on an aerial photograph and compare amount of green spaces noted on aerial maps from 20 years ago, 10 years ago, and on a current map. Students also discuss different types of land formation and soil types.

Opening Activity. What do you think was on the land where our school is 20 years ago? How could we find out? Is soil different in different areas? Discuss students responses and ideas.

In the chart below, write any of the below words or phrases that apply to each soil sample:

Texture/moisture: Rub the soil between your fingers. Choose words that describe how it feels:
- dry, moist, wet, very wet, or drippy, etc.
- falls apart, sticks together, sticky (sticks to fingers), etc.
- feels like clay (easily molded into shapes like modeling clay), slippery, oozes between fingers if you squeeze it, etc.

Soil particles: Draw the size and shape of the particles. What is the sample made of?
- sand (feels gritty)
- minerals (*tiny* bits of rocks)
- clay (like the cat litter sample)
- silt (like flour or powder; slippery when wet)
- pebbles
- organic matter (bits of leaves, twigs, bark, etc.)

Other features or creatures: What does the soil smell like? List or describe any rocks, dead plants, or other nonliving materials in the soil. List or describe any living things, such as worms, roots, or insects, in the soil. Do you see any roots with "rusty" red or orange soil around them?

Depth from soil surface	Texture/ moisture (describe how it feels)	Soil particles (describe or identify them)	Color # (use color chart)	Other features or creatures
2 in. or 5 cm				
4 in. or 10 cm				
6 in. or 15 cm				
12 in. or 30 cm				
18 in. or 45 cm				

Figure 3.3. Dig In: Part II
SOURCE: *WOW!: The Wonders Of Wetlands.* (1995). Copyright Environmental Concern Inc., St. Michaels, MD, 410-745-9620; and the Watercourse/Project WET, Bozeman, MT, 506-994-1917. Reprinted with permission.

Lesson Activities
1. Look at aerial photograph from 20 years ago and locate school grounds. Discuss green space where school is now and surrounding area.
2. Explain and discuss different land types, including mountains, deserts, rivers, meadows, and marshes.
3. Ask students to eliminate land types that do not fit the description of their school land.
4. Read "Dig In: Part II" (*WOW!: The Wonders Of Wetlands*) with students.
5. Walk outside and dig a soil sample, following the directions in "Dig In," with students feeling, smelling, and examining the soil.

Closing Activity. Did the soil meet the criteria for a wetland? How do you know? Discuss responses with table groups.

Materials
1. Aerial photographs of school area (current, 10 years old, 20 years old—may be borrowed from county planning department)
2. "Dig In: Part II" activity page from *WOW!: The Wonders Of Wetlands*
3. Small shovel for digging soil
4. Pictures depicting each land type (mountains, desert, marsh, etc.)

Lesson #5: Creatures of the Wetland

Objective. Students observe, count, sketch, and write a short story about the "creature population" in the front yard.

Opening Activity. Remember from the aerial map all the green space that was here 10 years ago? Where did the animals go that lived there? What kind of creature would live there? Write student responses on overhead and discuss ideas with class.

Lesson Activities
1. Read *Between Cattails* by Terry T. Williams. Discuss the kind of creatures found in the story.

Photo 3.2. Nalani and Students Surveying Wetland

2. Explain that today we will inspect the front yard for creatures and their habitats. How do scientists act when they are trying to find out about animals in their natural habitat? What will you do if you see a creature? Is an insect a creature? Is a bird a creature? How about a slug?

3. Each student will use a magnifying glass and carry his or her "research" clipboard with paper for drawing sketches of creatures and habitats, taking notes, and keeping track of certain creatures.

4. On returning to the classroom, students discuss the different creatures they observed and list the name of the creature (or add a tally if the name is already listed) on a large sheet of butcher paper.

Closing Activity. Discuss the following questions: "How many creatures did we see?" "Did we see all the creatures that live there?" "Why or why not?"

Materials
1. Williams, Terry T. (1985). *Between Cattails*

2. Magnifying glasses
3. Clipboards with paper and pencil
4. Butcher paper and pens

Lesson #6: What Lives in Water?

Objective. Students collect water samples from the wetlands and observe living organisms with the aid of a microscope.

Opening Activity. Discuss the following questions: "What lives in water?" "How can we find out what lives in water if it is too little to see?"

Lesson Activities
1. Read *The First Book of Swamps and Marshes* with the class. Discuss the living creatures that hide in the swamp and the smaller organisms that also live in water areas.
2. Each pair of students picks up a container with a lid to use to collect water from the wetlands.
3. Return with water sample to class, students going to microscope stations around room. Remind students how to adjust the knob for viewing.
4. Using an eye dropper, place water samples on slides for viewing. With young children, parent helpers or students from older classrooms would provide assistance with help in using the microscope.
5. After students have viewed their sample and located an organism, students draw the organism on a 3-inch square of paper and place paper on large sheet of butcher paper. The completed chart will be a quilt made up of all organisms found in the wetlands. Students will compare and contrast their organism(s) to others on the chart.
6. Using a chart of common water organisms, the students will find the names of several of the common organisms.

Closing Activity. Ask students to share with their neighbor one thing that made their organism similar to others and one thing that made their organism different.

Photo 3.3. Student Searching for Different Vegetation

Materials
1. Smith, Francis. (1969). *The First Book of Swamps and Marshes*
2. Containers for collecting water samples (2 to 6 ounces)
3. Microscopes
4. Three-inch squares of paper for illustrating water organisms
5. Butcher paper for quilt chart
6. Chart of common water organisms

Lesson #7: Vegetation Growing in Our Wetland

Objective. Students identify several natural wetland plants and explain one function that plants provide in a wetlands area.

Opening Activity. Ask students to think about the plants in the school yard and about characteristics that make plants look different from each other. Generate a list from their ideas on the overhead projector.

Lesson Activities
1. On the overhead projector, place a transparency made from a page of common wetland plants growing in this region. Dis-

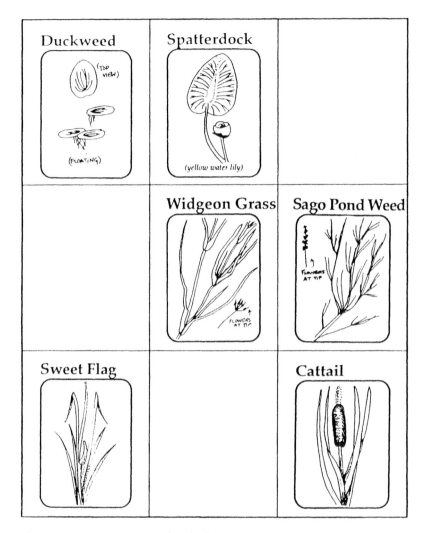

Figure 3.4. Common Wetland Plants

SOURCE: *WOW!: The Wonders Of Wetlands.* (1995). Copyright Environmental Concern Inc., St. Michaels, MD, 410-745-9620; and the Watercourse/ Project WET, Bozeman, MT, 506-994-1917. Reprinted with permission.

cuss the similarities and differences of these plants, noting leaf shape, size, and structure; color of plant; flowers of plant; size of plant; and other characteristics.

2. Each child has a clipboard with both the same page of plants and blank sections included for drawing his or her diagrams of plants. The class walks to the wetlands area in the front of

Photo 3.4. The Celery Experiment: Some Stalks Are Turning Brown

the school and identifies plants shown on the plant page or draws plants that are not shown.

3. After returning to the classroom, students will share their findings with a small group, attempting to identify plants that they found outside.

4. Read *Desert* by Clint Twist and discuss purpose and living conditions of plants in other regions and in wetland areas.

5. Mix a solution of brown water with food coloring and water. Pour about 4 to 6 ounces of the brown water into a cup for each student. Explain that the brown water will be like muddy water. Each student will place a celery stalk in the water and will check the water and celery in the morning to note any change.

Closing Activity. Each small group draws a plant, names the plant, and posts the drawing on the board. The whole class views the drawings on the board and notes commonalities and differences between the plants.

Materials
1. Transparency and copies of common plants handout found in local wetlands area

2. Clipboard with pencil
3. Copy of page of common plants on clipboard
4. Pens and crayons for drawing
5. Food coloring for brown water
6. Cups (clear plastic) for celery experiment
7. Stalk of celery for each child
8. Twist, Clint. (1991). *Desert*

Lesson #8: Purpose of Wetlands[1]

Objective. Students use metaphors to describe basic conditions and purposes of wetlands.

Opening Activity. Students check their celery and brown water experiment and record their findings in their journal. The class discusses journal entries and findings. The findings become hypotheses for purposes of plants in wetlands. Then ask the class to close their eyes and picture the wetland in front of the school. What animals and other creatures live there? What plants are found there?

Lesson Activities
1. Share and discuss images students noted about the wetland in the opening activity.
2. Provide the following background information about the basic ecological activities occurring in wetlands:
   a. Sponge effect—provides runoff control
   b. Filter effect—takes out silt, toxins, wastes, and so on (relate to celery and brown water experiment)
   c. Nutrient control—absorbs nutrients from fertilizers and other sources that may cause contamination
   d. Natural nursery—provides shelter and food for newborn wildlife
3. Divide students into groups of four for the following activity. Have the "Mystery Metaphor Container" ready (a box filled with a sponge, a small pillow, soap, an egg beater, a toy cradle, a fan, a strainer or sieve, a bag of pretzels). Present the idea that each item has something to do with a wetland. Each group sends one student to the box to select an item.

4. Each group discusses the relationship between its object and the wetland.

5. Groups share their ideas with the entire class and listen to other groups' thoughts on the connection between their object and wetlands.

6. Have the class summarize the major roles that wetlands perform in contributing to a healthy environment. Record their ideas on a butcher paper chart for future reference.

Closing Activity. Discuss how wetlands and their functions depend on and affect humans. After a discussion, students write in their journal one way that they can help wetlands, or they draw an illustration of their idea in their journal.

Materials
1. Box or bag
2. Sponge
3. Strainer or sieve
4. Pillow
5. Toy cradle
6. Bar of soap
7. Egg beater
8. Fan
9. Pretzels
10. Student journals

Lesson #9: What Should We Do With Our Front Yard?

Objective. Students work with their small group to develop a proposal for the front yard of the school and prepare a video segment presenting research conducted on the wetlands area.

Opening Activity. Ask students to think about the different research areas that they have completed with the wetlands study. When they have decided what area is of most interest to them, they are to sign up on the job chart and be responsible to work with a group to develop their interest into a taped segment for the video production about the use of the school's front yard.

Photo 3.5. Scientists Making Finds During Wetland Investigation

Lesson Activities
1. Students spend time with their work group to determine how they will present their research on their topic of interest.
2. When the groups have developed their plan, the teacher will tape their presentation. Visual aids are strongly encouraged (use of quilt chart, celery experiment, charts created from discussions, pictures of plants or animals in the wetlands, etc.).
3. Final segment of tape presents students' solutions to the problem of deciding what to do with the front yard of the school.
4. Teacher and students edit tape and arrange for local school committee, parents, administrators, county planners, and others to attend presentation.

Closing Activity. Groups share progress and ask for peer assistance with graphics, visual aids, or other areas if needed.

Materials
1. Charts, experiments, objects from prior lessons
2. Video camera

Photo 3.6. Poem Created by Second Graders About Wetland Creatures

Note: This lesson may take several days to complete.

Lesson #10: Sharing Our Solution With the Community

Objective. Students present their research findings and conclusions to community members who are also affected by the use or misuse of the front yard of the school.

Opening Activity. Students take the audience to the front yard of the school, asking them to observe this area and then return to the school.

Lesson Activities
1. Students begin presentation by talking about the problem of what to do with the front yard of the school.
2. Students show video production and engage the audience in a discussion about what they viewed.
3. Students share with the audience the experiments, research findings, charts, and other research they have compiled.

4. At the end of the presentation, students lead a tour of the wetland, describing the animal and plant life and the many functions of the wetland.

5. Students ask everyone to think how they can help preserve important wetland areas so the wetlands will still be there when they are adults.

Closing Activity. Students review their journal entries and reflect on their learning about wetlands, then write in their journals about their impression of their learning growth about wetlands.

Unit Resources

Children's Literature

Buch, L. (1974). *Wetlands: Bogs, Marshes and Swamps.* New York: Parents Magazine Press.

Carrick, C., & Carrick, D. (1969). *Swamp Spring.* New York: Macmillan.

Cowing, S. (1980). *Our Wild Wetlands.* New York: J. Messner.

Freschet, B. (1974). *Year on Muskrat Marsh.* New York: Scribner.

Gemming, E. (1983). *The Cranberry Book.* New York: Coward-McCann.

Linn, C. (1976). *The Everglades: Exploring the Unknown.* Muhwah, NJ: Troll Associates.

Matthew, D. (1994). *Wetlands.* New York: Simon & Schuster.

Smith, F. C. (1969). *The First Book of Swamps and Marshes.* New York: Franklin Watts.

Stone, L. (1989). *Wetlands.* Vero Beach, FL: Rourke Enterprises.

Twist, C. (1991). *Deserts.* New York: Dillon.

Williams, T. (1985). *Between Cattails.* New York: Scribner.

Films/Videos

Conserving America: Wetlands. National Wildlife Federation.

The Marsh Community. Encyclopedia Britannica Educational Corporation.

Curriculum Guides

Lynn, B. (1988). *Discover Wetlands.* Olympia: Washington State Department of Ecology.

National Wildlife Federation. (1989). *Nature Scope: Wading Into Wet-lands*. Washington, DC: Author.

U.S. Fish and Wildlife Service. (1987). *Project Wild: Aquatic*. Bethesda, MD: Western Regional Environmental Education Council.

WOW!: The Wonders Of Wetlands. (1995). St. Michaels, MD: Environmental Concern Inc.

Yates, S. (1989). *Adopting a Wetland: A Northwest Guide*. Olympia, WA: Snohomish County Planning and Community Development.

Summary of Our Front Yard

Throughout this unit, students were involved in social studies as they explored (a) the history and effect of people on the wetland and the effect of the wetland on people; (b) mathematics through charting, graphing, tallying, and measuring the wetland and its content; (c) literature through reading about wetland areas, writing in their journals and recording data, and communicating with experts in wetland management; (d) technology when using scientific equipment to take water samples and study soil samples, using computers for tapping into networks with current information about wetlands, and using camcorders to document their work; (e) art as they drew the wildlife, plants, and maps of the wetlands area; and (f) science as they used the scientific method to study the wetlands and gain knowledge about the environmental impact on and from wetland regions.

Although the students and teacher at this school had a wetlands area in their school yard, the unit could be adapted to any elementary school with a wetland within field trip distance. In the Portland region, each school has adapted a "green space" within walking distance of the school. This green space could serve as a context for real-world problem solving.

Students without access to a wetland might examine problems associated with a land space in their area, such as a desert area, mountain range, river, lake, stream, or some shrinking or endangered land space within the city or on the outskirts of a city. Students could develop a "problem" that requires in-depth investigation and research as they explore land usage. Preferably, the land or area to be studied would be within walking distance of the school to enable students to make several trips to study vegetation, animal life,

Photo 3.7. Model of School and Wetland

changes occurring during the time period, and the effects of land on people and people on land. If the land to be studied is not nearby, one alternative is to make use of extensive videotaping and photographs taken during the first visit to the land space. Subsequent trips could continue to use photography, drawings, and videotaping throughout the unit to remind students of the vegetation, wildlife, soil, and topography as they continue their study of this land space. Data gathered during the initial visit could be analyzed, sorted, categorized, and compared to findings in later visits. Land usage remains an important issue in our lives, and student research will contribute to future decisions affecting humans, animals, plants, and land, essentially quality-of-life decisions.

SABIN ELEMENTARY SCHOOL
AND THE PROBLEM OF SHOES

This unit was taught by Susan Duncan, intern teacher, to a class of 27 fifth graders at Sabin Elementary School in the Portland Public School District. Sabin is an inner-city school located in a residential neighborhood in Northeast Portland. There are 630 students in the

Photo 3.8. Trying on Buck Williams's Shoes, Donated by Portland TrailBlazers

school, in grades from prekindergarten through grade 5. More than 60% of the student body is composed of African American students. The three-story, brick school was built in 1928. Parents and the community are active in the school, as evidenced in the band program taught by local musicians with donated band instruments and the volunteers working with different school-related projects.

The fifth-grade classroom is located on the third floor of the northwest corner of the building. Students sit in groups of four or five, with desks pushed together to facilitate team or group work. Several volunteers work in the classroom throughout the week, either with students or with tasks associated with student work or projects. Although most of the day is spent in the classroom with the teacher, students do move to the gymnasium for physical education, the library for literature and library skills, and to music for band or vocal music on a weekly schedule. Recess is outside on a large playing field, with a section that is covered for play on rainy days.

Choosing Shoes and Making Sense and Cents

Unit Overview. Shoes are common, everyday items owned by most people in our country. We usually choose our own shoes, making a purchase decision based on style, brand, or comfort. The real-world problem that is the focus of this unit explores shoes and choosing shoes. How do shoe construction and production affect natural, human, and economic resources? What can be learned about shoes that might impact our decisions when choosing shoes?

Unit Goals. Students develop an understanding of how shoes are made, what function shoes serve, how resources are affected by shoe manufacturing, and consumer influence on production and use of resources.

Unit Activities
1. Examine the function of a shoe and share a story written from the perspective of a shoe.
2. Estimate the area of an irregular shape and determine the cost of materials to construct a shoe of that shape.
3. Research the cost and source of several materials that might be used in shoe construction.
4. Describe the difference between a renewable and a nonrenewable resource.
5. Draw and explain a production graph.
6. Conduct research to determine a suitable shoe design.
7. Identify advantages of a product from a consumer's perspective.
8. Research influence of climate and environment on shoe design.
9. Create a flowchart depicting materials from the original source to the completed shoe.

10. Develop a promotional campaign for a shoe design.

11. Explain both the problem the newly designed shoe resolves and benefits of the new product.

Lesson #1: Parts of a Shoe

Objective. Students examine and name the different parts of shoes.

Opening Activity. Ask students to individually brainstorm and record the name for each part of a shoe.

Lesson Activities
1. Make a composite list of shoe parts on the chalkboard.
2. Have students take off one of their shoes and look for the different parts according to the class list.
3. Explain that most shoes have the same parts and shoemakers have developed terms to identify these parts.
4. List these terms on the overhead: *toe cap, vamps, apron, tongue, heel, lace, sole, quarter, counter, buckle, lining, welt.*
5. Ask students to work with a partner and find as many of these parts as possible.
6. Using a diagram of a shoe, have students complete the parts diagram on the overhead projector.
7. In groups of four, give each student a picture with only one part of a shoe. They are to find the rest of the shoe, using the vocabulary they worked with today, and make a whole shoe within their group.

Closing Activity. Discuss which parts of the shoes are on every shoe and which parts might be only on some shoes. Why or why not?

Materials
1. Shoes (could use shoes that students are wearing)
2. Diagram of shoe for overhead
3. List of shoemaker's terminology for shoe parts on transparency

Lesson #2: A Shoe's View

Objective. Students describe the many functions of shoes.

Opening Activity. What is one word that your shoe would say if it could talk?

Lesson Activities
1. Read a section of *Striding Slippers* by M. Ginsburg, asking the students to think of the story from the shoe's view.
2. Within a group of four, each student becomes one part of a shoe and tells the portion of the story from that view.
3. Ask students to place the shoes they brought from home on their desks. Ask them to look at the shoe and think up a story to tell about the life of this shoe.
4. Students discuss their ideas with each other and begin the rough draft of their story about the life of their shoe. Some questions to consider are the following: "Who wore this shoe?" "Where was it made?" "What would a normal day be for this shoe?" "Where has the shoe been?" "Has the shoe needed repairs?"

Closing Activity. Place all shoes on a table or window ledge. Ask students how old the shoes are all together. How far have they traveled? Discuss their ideas about the answers and how to find the answers with the class.

Materials
1. Ginsburg, Mirra. (1978). *Striding Slippers*
2. A shoe from home for each child
3. Paper and pencils for writing

Lesson #3: Area of a Shoe

Objective. Students estimate the area of a shoe sole, giving an answer in square centimeters.

Opening Activity. Hold up a piece of square centimeter paper. Ask the class how we would find out the number of centimeter squares on the page without counting each square. Discuss ideas with class.

Lesson Activities

1. Each child has a piece of square centimeter paper. With his or her partner's help, they trace the sole of their shoe onto the paper.
2. How do you find out how many centimeters are in the sole of your shoe? Discuss ideas with whole class.
3. Each student estimates, then counts the number of centimeters that cover the sole of his or her shoe on the paper.
4. Discuss how the portions of centimeter squares were counted. (Usually students put two "pieces" of centimeter squares together and count as one, or three pieces if smaller.) Share ideas with class.
5. Talk about shoe production and the best use of resources to save money. With shoe soles, if the shoemaker has a piece of leather, the object would be to obtain the greatest number of shoe soles with the smallest amount of leftover material.
6. Each child cuts out his or her shoe sole from the centimeter paper.
7. Each student lays the shoe sole on a piece of construction paper (11 × 14) and traces the sole, making as many soles as possible from the one sheet of paper.
8. Students collect their leftover pieces of paper and measure them on an uncut piece of centimeter paper, trying to determine if they could have wasted less of that resource.

Closing Activity. If each square centimeter represents 10 cents of resource material, how much did the leftovers from your shoe sole cost?

Materials

1. Shoe
2. Square centimeter paper
3. Construction paper (11 × 14)
4. Scissors

Lesson #4: Resources and Shoes

Objective. Students describe different resources and materials used in making shoes.

Opening Activity. What are shoes made out of? Make a list on the chalkboard of student ideas.

Lesson Activities
1. Each group chooses a shoe from the front of the room. (There are five shoes or pictures of shoes representing shoes made of cotton, wool, synthetics, leather, and wood.)
2. The group researches the major material of their shoe from original source (i.e., rubber from a rubber tree) to the finished shoe. Students access books, encyclopedias, and the computer resources for research references.
3. Each group develops a flowchart to depict the sequence of material development and the effect on the environment (air, water, forests, etc.).
4. Each group presents their flowchart to the entire class, explaining the process from raw material to finished shoe.
5. The class groups the five shoe materials into two groups: renewable resources and nonrenewable resources.

Closing Activity. Students write in their journals about one of the shoe materials and the pros and cons for using this material for mass production of shoes.

Materials
1. Butcher paper and pens for flowcharts
2. Five shoes (leather, cotton, wood, synthetics, wool) or pictures of such shoes
3. Journals

Lesson #5: Our Shoe Company

Objective. Students develop a production graph and explain the rate of production of their shoe company.

Photo 3.9. Experimenting With Shoe-Making Resources

Opening Activity. Ask the students to think of an answer to the following questions: "Is it faster for one person to make a whole shoe or for each person to specialize in making one part of the shoe and sending it on to the next specialist?" "Why or why not?"

Lesson Activities
1. Hold up a completed baby shoe and explain the steps taken to make the shoe from a kit.
2. Record the steps to completing the shoe on the chalkboard.
3. Half the class receives one complete shoe kit with instructions.
4. The other half of the class receives shoe parts and works in an assembly line to complete the shoes. Students work together to decide on assembly line jobs and job descriptions.
5. Each student records the time started and the time stopped at the beginning and end of each time period he or she works on shoe construction.

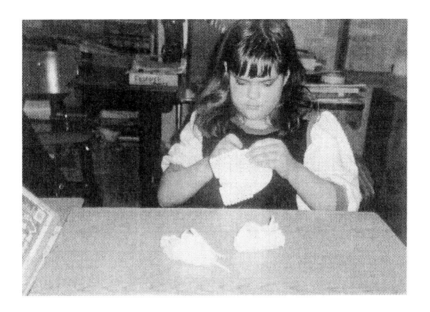

Photo 3.10. Making Shoes: Individual Versus Factory Process

6. After completion of all shoes, students chart the amount of time the assembly line needed to complete the 14 pairs of shoes and divide this time by 14 (the number of shoe pairs).

7. All the individual shoemakers add their time together and divide by 13 (the number of people in the group) to reach the average length of time to complete one pair of shoes.

8. Each student makes a graph of the production rates, selecting either a bar chart, a pie chart, or another form for representation of the data.

9. Students share production graphs with group, explaining their pictorial representation of the data.

Closing Activity. Ask students to discuss with their neighbor the advantages and disadvantages of both individual production and group assembly production.

Materials
1. Baby shoe kits (one for each student)

Photo 3.11. Creative Uses for Old Shoes

2. Graph paper and pens

Lesson #6: Who Decides What Your Shoes Will Look Like?

Objective. Students describe the work of a marketing researcher and provide two examples of how shoe design was impacted by environment or popular interest.

Opening Activity. Ask the students what a theme board is and what would be on a theme board. Brainstorm all possibilities.

Lesson Activities
1. Discuss a possible job description of a marketing researcher interested in finding out what kind of shoes people want to wear. The following information might be helpful in describing the job: collects data about people's favorite colors, recreational activities, and entertainment (i.e., characters in books or

movies, television shows, etc.); age and gender of potential consumer; interests and hobbies.

2. Ask students to think why this information would be helpful to a company when they are designing new shoes.

3. Each student has now been hired as a designer and develops a theme board to help create a shoe that would appeal to teenagers. Show them a sample theme board and discuss the different pictures on the board.

4. Invite a local designer to come to the school and share several theme boards with the class.

5. Each student (or team of students) selects a picture representing a specific time period and different country where their shoe design will be marketed. Students then research the climate, available resources, lifestyles, interests and activities, and other information unique to this time and place.

6. The theme board is created with pictures, swatches of material, index cards with information, and other pertinent material helpful for matching a shoe design with the needs of this group of people.

7. Students present and explain their theme boards to the class.

Closing Activity. Students write or draw in their journal about their theme board and a shoe design that would be appropriate for their group of people, including a rationale.

Materials
1. Tag board
2. Index cards
3. Fabric, other material swatches
4. Pictures representing different eras (one for each student or team of students)

Lesson #7: Publicity and the Consumer

Objective. Students describe how a sales campaign might affect people's decisions when purchasing shoes.

Opening Activity. Open today's newspaper and ask students to choose an advertisement that appeals to them. Discuss possible reasons why this advertisement is included in the newspaper. List their ideas on the board.

Lesson Activities
1. Provide each student with a magazine or newspaper and ask them to cut out an advertisement that appeals to them or one that makes them read the advertisement closer.
2. Have students share the advertisements they selected and their reasoning for choosing the advertisement with their group.
3. Students create an advertisement for the shoe they designed in the prior lesson. Remind students to include enough information about the product so the people know what they are buying. Students may use video, still camera, artwork, narratives, posters, newspaper or magazine ads, or other forms of advertising.
4. Videotape the students' work and make a tape of the advertisements.

Closing Activity. Ask students to discuss the following question in their journals: "What makes you want to buy something new that you have not tried before?"

Materials
1. Newspapers
2. Magazines
3. Camcorder
4. Camera
5. Journals

Lesson #8: What Shoe Makes Sense and Cents?

Objective. Students evaluate many pairs of shoes and select one pair based on best use of resources, comfort, design, length of wear of shoe, and cost.

Opening Activity. Ask the students to think of several responses to this question: "How do we decide what to buy?" Share their responses with the class and discuss ideas.

Lesson Activities
1. Explain that each group will decide what pair of shoes to buy, based on the research findings prior to this lesson. Students might consider use of resources, appeal, design, use for shoes, cost, longevity of shoes, and other influential factors.
2. Each group develops a list of required standards for its shoe purchase.
3. Students research existing shoes based on purchasing considerations and either select an existing shoe or design a shoe that meets their standards.
4. A shoe buyer from a local company visits the class and talks about considerations she works with in making purchasing decisions.
5. Each group creates a poster or other visual about "their shoe that makes sense and cents" and writes a justification paper to accompany the poster.

Closing Activity. Students invite other classes and the principal to visit their class and view the posters.

Materials
1. Poster paper
2. Pens
3. Paint

Unit Resources

Children's Literature

Anderson, H. C. (1983). *The Red Shoes.* Boston: Neugebauer.
Badt, K. (1994). *On Your Feet.* Chicago: Children's Press.
Bailey, D. (1991). *Shoes.* Toronto: Annick.
Corey, D., & Leder, D. (1985). *New Shoes!* Niles, IL: A. Whitman.
Galdone, P. (1976). *Puss in Boots.* New York: Seabury.
Ginsburg, M. (1978). *Striding Slippers.* New York: Macmillan.

Grimm, J., Grimm, W., & Aduno, A. (1960). *The Shoemaker and the Elves*. New York: Scribner.

Hurwitz, J. (1993). *New Shoes for Silvia*. New York: Morrow Junior Books.

Rowland, D. (1989). *A World of Shoes*. Chicago: Contemporary Books.

Roy, R., & Hausherr, R. (1988). *Whose Shoes Are These?* New York: Clarion.

Travers, P. L., Dillon, L., & Dillon, D. (1980). *Two Pairs of Shoes*. New York: Viking.

Video

Donahue, J. C. (1985). *The Red Shoes*. MCA Home Video, Inc.

Summary of Which Shoe to Choose?

Susan and her students developed this unit around shoes, an everyday item. The problem is found in the use of resources and the impact of consumerism on the environment. Instead of starting with the problem of overuse of natural and nonrenewable resources, the unit revolves around decision making in purchasing shoes and how each person's decision affects many parts of the world.

The real-world problem of decision making when purchasing items is one that all consumers face. Becoming an informed citizen who is able to make wise decisions regarding recycling, purchases, critical voting issues, and use of limited resources is an important goal as we approach the 21st century. Through the real-world problem solving of making sound decisions about purchases, students are engaged in learning about issues and concerns they will be faced with as adults. These are important decisions, as the students recognized when they developed their own shoe designs and purchasing decisions.

Many of the lessons in this unit evolved over a period of several weeks. There was a great deal of research to complete, and findings were essential in the scope of the problem solving. Students were amazed to find the difference in assembly work and in individual work when making baby shoes. Several of the assembly line workers were not sure they would want a job where they did the same task day after day. This made for a lively discussion about careers. Students began examining their own possessions, talked about wise purchases,

Photo 3.12. Potential Shoe Design of the Future

and shared discussions that had taken place at home about purchases. It was enlightening to watch their interest in commercialism and advertising grow. The real-world problem of decision making in everyday purchases certainly brings relevant and meaningful learning into the classroom.

Related items that other students might be interested in using as a focus for their problem solving might include clothing, cars, bicycles, toys, items for a home, items used at school (e.g., pencils and the depletion of forests to provide wood for pencils), or food. A class of students might decide to break up into small groups and each look at problem solving with a different object or examine and research different problems surrounding the same item. The closer the item is to the students' interest, the more invested the students become as they research different aspects of the manufacturing and the effects on our environment caused by manufacturing a specific item.

CATLIN GABEL SCHOOL:
COEXISTENCE OF SALMON AND HUMANS

The Catlin Gabel School is an independent day school with 648 students enrolled in preschool through grade 12. The school is located on the west side of Portland, approximately 5 miles west of the downtown area, with students traveling from all regions of Portland to attend Catlin Gabel. The original occupants of the land deeded the 55 acres of farmland and buildings to the school, which was founded in 1957. In the Lower School, there are 201 students (Grades 1-5) and more than 30 faculty, including the specialty area teachers. The majority of students are from middle- to upper-class families, although the school has a commitment to creating a more diverse population.

The main building of the Lower School was recently remodeled and includes five homerooms, science and computer labs, kitchens, the headmaster's office, and faculty work space. The Lower School is situated in a wooded setting, with several play areas and a soccer field surrounding the school. Students walk to nearby buildings to attend classes in modern languages, art, music, woodshop, and physical education.

The fifth-grade classroom where this unit was taught is made up of one large room with eight tables for students, sitting five or six to a table. There is a movable room divider to separate the classroom into two areas when desired. Adjacent to the homeroom is a quiet workroom, a kitchen, and a computer lab with 14 computers. Forty-two students are in the fifth grade, with one fourth of the students from families with a parent working at Catlin. Some of the lessons were taught in the classroom; others in the science laboratory. The science lab is one large room with a worktable, tables for group work, sinks, a refrigerator, a stove, and an adjacent greenhouse.

Parents play an important role in the school and are encouraged to help with activities in the class, field trips, and special events. Conferences are held with each student's parents at least twice each school year and parents are involved in fund-raising and school-related events throughout the year.

Kim Bauer, the intern teacher, developed and taught this unit (humans and salmon) over a 20-week period. "Humans and Salmon: Can They Coexist" became a major focus for the fifth-grade year. As the unit evolved, it was integrated with a later unit on Northwest Coastal Native Americans.

Humans and Salmon:
Can They Coexist?

Unit Overview. As the human population and pollution increase, the number of salmon in the Northwest are diminishing rapidly. Students will explore causes for the dwindling number of salmon, the impact of salmon on humans and humans on salmon, consider if the salmon population should increase, and if so, propose recommendations to help the salmon survive.

Unit Goals. Students explore the interrelationship between salmon and humans and the historical and current importance of this interdependency.

Unit Activities
1. Examine survival needs of humans and survival needs of salmon.
2. Define the unique characteristics of a salmon.
3. Describe the external and internal body parts of a salmon and their functions.
4. Compare and contrast the salmon family: five Pacific salmon (chinook, coho, chum, pink, and sockeye) and two anadromous trout (cutthroat and steelhead).
5. Explain the salmon life cycle, from birth to death.
6. Describe and discuss hazards that salmon face at each stage of their life cycle.
7. Explain the relationship between water temperature and salmon egg development.
8. Describe the development and special characteristics of salmon embryos from fertilization to hatching.
9. Construct and solve possible dilemmas that impact wildlife.
10. Discuss and give an example of coexistence.
11. List threats to salmon and provide possible solutions to these threats.
12. Develop a presentation that depicts Northwest Coastal Native American life and the interdependency between salmon and the lifestyle of these groups.

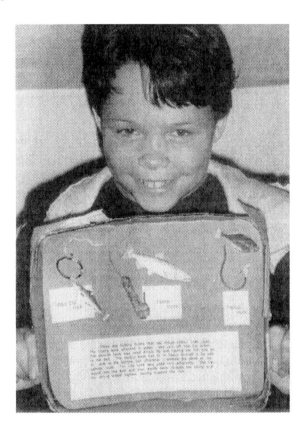

Photo 3.13. Impacts on Salmon Survival

13. Create a newspaper with articles about real-world problems linked to the interrelationship between humans and salmon.

Lesson #1: What Do You Need to Survive? What Do Salmon Need to Survive?

Objective. Students develop a list of survival needs of humans and survival needs of salmon.

Opening Activity. Students discuss what would happen if they were stranded in the woods and far away from other people. What do they need to survive? Brainstorm suggestions from the class and record on a sheet of butcher paper.

Lesson Activities
1. Ask the students to remember the book, *Island of the Blue Dolphin.* What did the main characters need to live? (Students had read this book in the beginning of the school year.)
2. Continue to add to the list of survival needs started at the beginning of the lesson.
3. Ask the students to think about salmon and what they might need to survive. Record all ideas on a second sheet of butcher paper. Accept all ideas, inviting students to research a topic of interest and add or delete ideas as the unit progresses.
4. Students select a book, magazine, or article about salmon and read a section. Following their reading, students share information in small groups.

Closing Activity. Review the two lists of survival needs (people and salmon) and ask students to identify similar needs and highlight these needs with a colored pen.

Materials
1. Butcher paper and pens
2. Books, magazines, articles about salmon

Lesson #2: What Makes a Salmon a Salmon?

Objective. Students describe the unique characteristics of a salmon.

Opening Activity. Ask the students to visualize a fish and picture one major characteristic specific to fish.

Lesson Activities
1. Place transparency of an external view of a salmon on the overhead. Using the reference sheet on salmon characteristics, ask students to identify and label each characteristic on the overhead and on their own worksheets. (Parts include dorsal

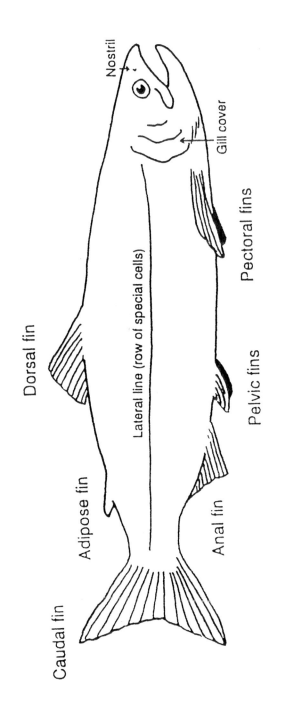

Figure 3.5. The External Anatomy of a Salmon
SOURCE: From *Salmonids in the Classroom* (1988). Reprinted with permission of the Department of Fisheries and Oceans, Ministry of Environment, Vancouver, B.C.

fin, caudal fin, adipose fin, pelvic fins, anal fin, pectoral fins, gill cover, lateral line, nostril, scales, mouth, gills, eye, tail, head, and body.)

2. Using the reference sheet, students discuss with the whole class the function of each characteristic and how this helps the salmon.

3. Each small group works with one characteristic of the external anatomy of the salmon and determines the function of the salmon part and the importance to fish survival.

Closing Activity. Ask students what would happen if the salmon had an accident with another salmon and was bitten on the pectoral fin. Discuss answers to the question.

Materials
1. Overhead transparency of salmon
2. Worksheets of salmon
3. Reference sheet with salmon characteristics and functions of characteristics

Lesson #3: Inside the Salmon

Objective. Students identify the major internal parts of a salmon and explain their basic functions.

Opening Activity. Talk to your neighbor about one internal part of your body that you think a salmon also has. What is the function of this body part?

Lesson Activities
1. Working in small groups, students identify and name internal body parts on the salmon worksheet.

2. Using the reference sheet, each small group also determines the function of each body part (e.g., the gill covers and the gill filaments work to force oxygen-containing water over the gills).

3. Students draw their own salmon, depicting both external and internal body parts.

Closing Activity. Which salmon body part is most like a human's body part? How are they alike and how are they different?

Materials
1. Reference page with salmon body parts and explanations of functions
2. Worksheets with salmon
3. Drawing paper

Lesson #4: The Salmon Family

Objective. Students discuss physical similarities and differences between the seven salmon species (chinook, coho, chum, pink, sockeye, steelhead, and cutthroat).

Opening Activity. Pass out a card representing one of the seven salmon species to each student. Ask the students to create a small group with other students who have the identical salmon on their card.

Lesson Activities
1. Students with the same species sit together and discuss the specific identifying features of their species, using the worksheets they had previously developed with external characteristics for reference to specific vocabulary (e.g., dorsal fin, pectoral fin, etc.).
2. Each group points out the distinguishing characteristics of its species to the class.
3. Using the overhead projector, display a salmon representing each species, asking the class to identify several distinguishing characteristics of each species.

Closing Activity. Referring to a large sheet of butcher paper listing the different distinguishing features of each species, ask students to look at their first worksheet and think about markings, gills, and so on that pertains to that species.

Materials
1. Cards (enough for one per student) representing one of the seven species of salmon

2. Overhead transparency of each of the seven species of salmon
3. Butcher paper and pens

Lesson #5: Life Cycle of Salmon

Objective. Students describe the life cycle of salmon.

Opening Activity. Ask the students, "What is a cycle?" Discuss and record student responses.

Lesson Activities
1. Students read about the salmon life cycle in *Discovering Salmon.*
2. List the following terms on the board: *egg, alevin, fry, smolt, adult,* and *spawner.*
3. Students draw a picture of the salmon at one stage of the life cycle, and then tape their pictures onto a chart representing all of the life stages.
4. Each group selects one of the six stages to work with in determining how the salmon is protected from predators at that specific stage. The group develops a short story to illustrate the protection provided at that life stage and shares with the class.

Closing Activity. Ask the students to think about "What makes a cycle a cycle?" Discuss the attributes of cycles.

Materials
1. Field, Nancy, & Machlis, Sally. (1984). *Discovering Salmon: A Learning and Activity Book*
2. Drawing paper and pens
3. Overhead transparency of life cycle of salmon

Lesson #6: Survival and Hazards in Salmon Life[2]

Objective. Students discover the hazards and survival rate at each step of the life cycle of salmon.

Opening Activity. Ask the students, "What might be life-threatening to a young salmon?" "Why?" Discuss the responses.

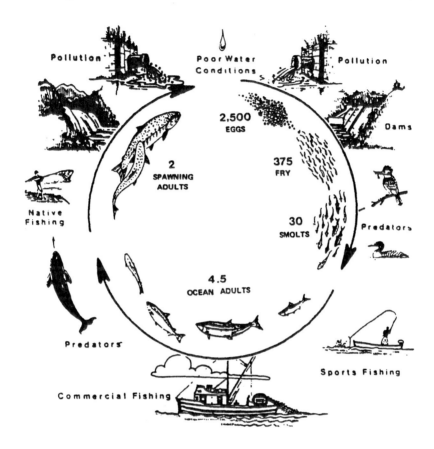

Figure 3.6. Hazards in the Life Cycle
SOURCE: From *Salmonids in the Classroom* (1988). Reprinted with permission of the Department of Fisheries and Oceans, Ministry of Environment, Vancouver, B.C.

Lesson Activities

1. Place the following information on the overhead: In the beginning, 2,500 eggs are waiting to develop into alevin. At the next stage, 375 fry are still alive. The next step, smolts, finds 30 of the original 2,500 alive. As ocean adults, 4.5 salmon remain alive, and at the final stage, spawning adults, only 2 salmon have made it to the final life stage. Ask students to think of all the hazards and dangers to salmon during their life cycle and list these hazards.

---

2. Develop a list of hazards (e.g., poor water conditions, pollution, dams, predators, and fishing).

3. Divide the class into six groups, numbering the groups one through six to represent six life cycle stages. Prove a large "pie slice" of butcher paper for each group to use in drawing a picture of the salmon at a specific life cycle stage and of hazards to the salmon at that stage, including the number of salmon alive at that stage of the life cycle.

4. Tape the pie slices together to make a whole circle and discuss the hazards and numbers of remaining salmon at each stage.

Closing Activity. Which stage is most hazardous to salmon? How could the survival rate improve?

Materials
1. Transparency with salmon life cycle information
2. "Hazards in the Life Cycle" handout
3. Butcher paper, pens, tape

Lesson #7: Water Temperature and Salmon Egg Development

Objective. Students describe the effect water temperature has on development of salmon eggs.

Opening Activity. Display a calendar with accumulated thermal units (ATUs) recorded over a 2-week period. Ask the students what they notice about the numbers on the calendar.

Lesson Activities
1. Gather the students at the large aquarium in the room. Ask them to read the thermometer in the tank. Write the temperature on the board and ask the students, "What does this number tell us?"

2. Explain that the temperature reading is for this moment but that we are also interested in the temperature of the tank water over a period of time, so we will be recording ATUs, which add the temperature from the second day to the temperature recorded on the first day. For example, Day 1 finds the ther-

Photo 3.14. Controlling Water Temperature for Optimal Egg Development

mometer reading 9° C. On the second day the thermometer reads 7° C, so the ATU is 16° C. ATU is used to keep track of the temperature and the predicted date for the hatching of the salmon eggs in the aquarium tank.

3. Using the calendar with prerecorded ATUs, ask the students to find the date the salmon eggs might hatch when the ATU reaches approximately 550 to 650° C. Ask students to explain their reasoning for predicting the date.

4. Post a calendar to use for recording ATUs in the classroom.

Closing Activity. Provide a calendar for each student and ask them to predict the week the salmon eggs will hatch in the classroom tank.

Materials
1. Aquarium tank
2. Thermometer
3. Calendar (large class calendar)
4. Calendar for each student

5. Fertilized salmon eggs for aquarium

Lesson #8: From Fertilization to Hatch[3]

Objective. Students explain the development of salmon embryo from fertilization to the hatch stage.

Opening Activity. Ask the students to think about babies, either human or animal babies, and the differences between a baby and someone their own age. Discuss their ideas and thoughts about dependence and development.

Lesson Activities
1. Watch video: *Birth of a Salmon.*
2. Discuss the imprinting of salmon to odors in the water. Why is this ability important to salmon?
3. Conduct a simulation of smell imprinting (the smell experiment), with six strong scents and six volunteer smellers. Put each of the six smelly objects or substances (e.g., banana peels, orange rind, coffee, onion, strong cheese, or perfume) on a cotton ball or, if possible, directly in a paper bag. Blindfold the six smellers and pair them with a partner who will lead them around the room. Each smeller is to sniff their object and name the object in their bag. The smellers then leave the room with their partners. The six bags are placed in different spots around the room. When the pairs return, the blindfolded smellers are to direct their partners to move them around the classroom until they smell their own bags. After the students find their bag or substance, ask them how they found the smell and what clues helped them identify their substance.
4. Ask students to think of reasons why salmon rely on smell to find their river. List and discuss all responses, relating the discussion to the smell experiment and the smell identification process the students used to find "their" substance.

Closing Activity. Each student briefly writes about the smell experiment and what could happen if the river the salmon were born in becomes polluted or altered in a significant way.

Photo 3.15. Students Recording in Portfolios

Materials
1. Video: *Birth of a Salmon.* (1988)
2. Video player
3. Six smelly substances
4. Paper bags
5. Cotton balls
6. Blindfolds

Lesson #9: Dilemmas and Wildlife

Objective. Students examine their personal beliefs about wildlife and consider the impact that each person makes on the environment.

Opening Activity. Students work in small groups to develop a dilemma faced by salmon or other wildlife. The dilemma represents a problem or situation that a student might encounter and requires decision making and a response by the student. For example, Jamie is walking home from school and notices other students throwing

Photo 3.16. Kim Releasing the Sole Surviving Salmon, Alvin

mud and debris into the creek near the school. Students in Jamie's class will be releasing the fry they have raised in the classroom into the creek in the next few days. The class had discussed water quality and experimented with imprinting and the importance of smell to salmon. What should Jamie do? After the dilemma scenarios are developed, each group switches dilemmas.

Lesson Activities
1. Small groups of students work together to discuss the dilemma and find possible solutions to the dilemma.
2. Students present their dilemma and solution to the whole class.

Closing Activity. Discuss the following questions: "Who has responsibility for protecting wildlife and the environment?" "What happens if each person decides someone else will take care of problems?"

Materials
1. Books, computer access, and resources for reference material for dilemmas

Lesson #10: Coexistence

Objective. Students describe a situation where coexistence occurs in a balanced manner.

Opening Activity. Brainstorm with the class on definitions of coexistence. Discuss and record ideas.

Lesson Activities
1. Each group draws a "role" from the basket. The roles represent different interest groups who are impacted by the declining number of salmon. Roles include farmer, Native American, forester, rancher, fisherman, and salmon.
2. Each group receives five acres of property with a stream running through the property. The group develops the land according to its needs for its livelihood. Students may create maps, videos, posters, or other visuals to represent their land and the changes they made to improve their livelihood.
3. Groups present their work to the whole class.
4. Each group is assigned to monitor another group's impact on the stream and salmon and develop a proposal that would help improve the stream for salmon habitat.

Closing Activity. Each student writes an essay or develops a visual presentation about one of the special interest group's impact on salmon.

Materials
1. Poster board, pens, paint
2. Clay and other supplies for the representation of property
3. Camcorder, blank videotapes

Lesson #11: Threats to Salmon

Objective. Students identify threats and potential threats to salmon.

Opening Activity. Ask the students to review their work on the life cycle of salmon and find three possible or potential threats to salmon.

Lesson Activities
1. Through a class discussion and review of previous lessons, list all possible threats to the salmon population.
2. Each small group selects two threats from the list.
3. The groups work together to problem solve and come up with possible solutions to these threats.
4. Groups share their ideas and solutions with the rest of the class.

Closing Activity. Ask students to think of two audiences they could communicate with about the threats to salmon and possible solutions. For homework, students write a letter to a group that has influence on the salmon population. The letters identify threats to salmon and suggested solutions.

Materials
1. Life cycle of salmon chart
2. Butcher paper and pens
3. Reference material about salmon

Lesson #12: Northwest Coastal Native Americans' Connection With Salmon

Objective. Students list and describe several connections or ties between Northwest Coastal Native Americans and salmon.

Opening Activity. Discuss the following with the students: Imagine that you lived near the coast in the Pacific Northwest many years ago. There were no grocery stores, banks, or cars. People were dependent on themselves and each other for food, housing, and other necessities. How would salmon be useful to these people? How would they feel toward an important food and life-giving source?

Lesson Activities
1. Discuss the books students have read about Northwest Coastal Native American life in the 1800s. Ask students to consider the following questions: "What did the Native Americans do for

Photo 3.17. Native American Fishing Village

recreation?" "Where did they find their food?" "How did they celebrate?"

2. Divide the class into three or more groups to research one of the preceding topics or any other topics the students generate about Northwest Coastal Native American life. Suggest that as they research their topics, students consider the contribution of salmon to these people.

3. Students spend a week or more gathering resources for their research and compiling a presentation for the class.

Closing Activity. Small-group presentations of Northwest Coastal Native American life and the connection with salmon to the whole class and students and staff from other classes.

Materials
1. Reference material about Northwest Coastal Native Americans

Lesson #13: *Production of the* Northwest News

Objective. Students research a current problem related to salmon and write an article for the *Northwest News* newspaper (class newspaper for this unit).

Opening Activity. Ask the students to think of the threats to salmon, hazards to salmon, people's reliance on salmon, and salmon's reliance on people. While students are thinking of these topics, ask them to select a problem related to salmon that they feel is important and would like to investigate further.

Lesson Activities
1. Following identification of a problem related to salmon, students may choose to work in small groups or individually to conduct their research. The research component may take several weeks to complete.
2. Ask students to bring interesting newspaper articles to read to the class about any topic. Students read the articles aloud and discuss the writing style and the author's ability and skills used to interest the reader in the topic. Begin compiling a list of skills or techniques used by newspaper writers in the examples read to the class.
3. Students write a draft of their article and assist each other in peer editing.
4. Students prepare a final draft of the article.

Closing Activity. Students print the newspaper and distribute it to the community. Personal letters are attached to several special interest group's newspapers.

Materials
1. Reference materials and resources about salmon
2. Software program to assist in developing the newspaper

Unit Resources

Literature

Cone, M. (1991). *Come Back, Salmon.* San Francisco: Sierra Club Books for Children.

Northwest News

Should the Native Americans be allowed to fish on their tribal fishing lands?

by Sequoia Medley & Rachel Greenough

June 1, 1994

"FISH: Serious condition of populations"
"COHO: 50 fish return to spawn from run that once numbered thousands"
"Low Coho return may halt '94 ocean season"
"Where have all the fish gone?"

Headlines like these from the Oregonian and other newspapers make the public more aware of the quickly declining salmon population. Some of the reasons for the low turnout for salmon this year are pollution and over fishing. Only two out of two thousand five hundred salmon will live to return home and spawn. Since many are caught on their way home less eggs are laid and thus fewer fish are born every year.

With the smaller salmon turnout the question of whether or not the Native Americans tribes like the Yakama, Umatilla, Warm Springs and the Nez Perce should be allowed to fish for salmon (which they use in ceremonies) on the Willamette River like their ancestors of long ago before the white settlers came.

We did a survey with the Catlin Gabel fifth grade and their teachers asking the question "What do you think about the shortage of salmon?"

Adrienne suggests "We should make the fishing of salmon illegal until there are more salmon"

Most people we asked agreed that something should be done about the shortage of salmon. Alyssa suggests " making a law so that if you are caught fishing for salmon you spend thirty years in prison."

We also asked the question "Do you think that the Native Americans should be allowed to fish on their tribal waters" Nine out of ten of those interviewed thought that the Native Americans should be allowed. Many People agreed with Kim Bauer the fifth grade intern in saying

" Most definitely it was their land in the beginning!" While an a unnamed source disagrees by saying "If other people can't fish there why should the Native Americans?"

In almost every case people shared the same general feelings that the Native Americans should have first priority in fishing. Others though feel that for there to be enough fish to go around we need some regulations.

Salmon fishing: limited or unlimited?

By Alyssa Webley

Salmon fishing has two sides. One side says that it should be limited the other side, mostly made of commercial fisherman, say we should have no limit. First we'll hear from the people that say it should be limited.

According to Portland area teacher, Kim Bauer, "There are so few salmon that it should be limited. I don't think fishing should be stopped all together but you know."

"I also think fishing should be limited because we're running out of salmon and if we keep fishing they'll be gone forever. One day we might get them back, but it's sad," says Catlin Gabel student, Rachel Greenough.

"I think it should be limited now," Adrienne Tozier thinks "Because if we have it limited for a while, then salmon will come back in numbers, Then it won't need to be limited."

Now you can hear from another side, Commercial fisherman. George Hickerman says this, "I think we should be able to fish as much as we want. How else will we live? We won't have any food. Fish is one of the top selling items of the market. All fisherman will be unemployed and this nation will have a high unemployment rate, our economy will then fall."

Another commercial fisherman named Tom Frowzier says, "We need more food in this economy, I don't want this world to go through another depression. Who cares about the fish? They'll never know a thing after we catch them. I propose we fish as much as we want."

One more person with the name, John Daniels, says that he thinks we should have it so only commercial fisherman are allowed to fish the salmon, the rest don't need to.

Today Mr. Clinton is proposing a rule that would protect all Salmon in Western Washington, Western Oregon and Northern California by restricting grazing, logging and road building along salmon streams.This would stay for 18 months.

There may be no Ocean Salmon fishing season this year, because out of 40 million only 13,000 fish came back, when they expected 49,000.

Dwindling Fish Population

By Joseph W.

The Salmon population is dwindling and the Government is not doing enough.

The Salmon run has been smaller then usual and in the words of The Oregonian,"The bad news just got worse." or in other words "We're past the mid point in the run and we only get 30 percent (of average count) in May". Because the avorage number of fish climbing the fish laders is19,000 but this year it is only 12,257.

"The commercial fishermen are fishing beyond what is safe." So make a limit on the maximum fish a company can catch and sell." said fish expert Joey Haber. If people want to fish on boats there is no reason to catch five fish and only eat one So why not Catch And Release.

But what can we do about it?"I think they should make it a law with a consequence" said Joey Haber. The not reenforced law that was that started 15 years ago requiring people to put screens over pips that go to irrigation systems so fish would not get sucked into the irrigation. What I think we should do is have some people raise money to buy the screens and attach them. Then prohibit fishing until the fishe's population is safe and then limit the fishing so that this does not happen again.

Figure 3.7. First Edition of *Northwest News*
SOURCE: Reprinted with permission of Kim Bauer's fifth-grade class.

Field, N., & Machlis, S. (1984). *Discovering Salmon: A Learning and Activity Book.* Corvallis, OR: Dog-Eared Publications.

Field, N., & Machlis, S. (1990). *Discovering Endangered Species: A Learning and Activity Book.* Corvallis, OR: Dog-Eared Publications.

Guiberson, B. (1993). *Salmon Story.* New York: Henry Holt.

Hayes, W. (1961). *About the Biggest Salmon.* Chicago: Melmont.

Hogan, P. (1979). *The Life Cycle of the Salmon.* Milwaukie, IL: Raintree Childrens Books.

Netboy, A. (1974). *The Salmon: Their Fight for Survival.* Boston: Houghton Mifflin.

Schemenauer, E. (1986). *Salmon.* Toronto: Grolier.

Wheeler, J. (1990). *The Animals We Live With.* Edina, MN: Abdo and Daughters.

Williamson. H. (1990). *The Illustrated Salar the Salmon.* Boston: Godine.

Video

Birth of a Salmon. (1988). Vancouver, BC: Department of Fisheries and Oceans.

Curriculum Guides

Project Wild: Aquatic. (1987). Bethesda, MD: Western Regional Environmental Education Council.

Salmonids in the Classroom. (1988). Vancouver, BC: Department of Fisheries and Oceans.

Summary of Salmon and Humans: Can They Coexist?

Throughout this unit, students found themselves becoming increasingly concerned about salmon and their dwindling population. The need to pay attention to environmental problems was clearly evident. Students found themselves becoming vocal about erosion of stream and river banks, overfishing of salmon, construction of new buildings near rivers, water pollution, and ranching near rivers. Many of these issues were known to the students before the unit, but the focus on survival of the salmon and the impact of people on the salmon population caused students to look at these issues with a

Photo 3.18. First Edition of *Northwest News*

grounded sense of concern for survival of a species. The issues became relevant and meaningful to the students as they learned more about the coexistence of and interrelationship between salmon and humans.

Students studied mathematics (temperature, land maps, population numbers, percentages related to survival), language arts (reading about salmon, Native Americans, writing a research report and newspaper article, writing letters to special interest groups), science (survival, hazards, threats, environmental science, etc.), art (Native American art, drawing and painting projects and visual aids), economics (decision making in politics based on limited resources), social studies (history of the area, influence of culture on land usage and lifestyle), and communication skills (presentations and interactions with community members). All of these disciplines were integrated as students gained new knowledge and applied the knowledge in projects and research about salmon and humans. The integrative approach to teaching and learning allowed students to explore topics around the problem of the coexistence of salmon and humans, with the purpose of acquiring knowledge and information that would lead to solving an important problem.

Students were empowered to conduct research and look at many sides of an issue while bringing critical information to the whole group. The final projects (presentations about interdependency between humans and salmon and creating the *Northwest News* newspaper) represented work and learning the students had completed over a 5-month period.

These fifth-grade students look at life with a different perspective now. Water quality takes on more importance. Although pollution and recycling were important prior to this unit, students now have a deeper understanding of the impact humans have on their environment. These ideas and many others have now become a part of the larger picture and relate to the real-world problem raised in the coexistence of salmon and humans.

Other students might be interested in exploring problems surrounding the balance between humans and wildlife or plants in their region. For example, changing long-term agricultural areas to industrial areas affects wildlife dependent on certain plants for their food and habitat. Students in urban schools might be curious to study the dependence (or interdependence) between specific plants and a bird population. Without access to certain flowers, some birds will not return to an area where they had previously dwelled. Students might also be interested in planting flowers or plants that would attract a species of birds or butterfly. Another group of students might be interested in looking at bird habitats and designing and building bird houses to attract birds into their neighborhood.

On a global level, students might wish to explore whales and the effect of whaling on the population of specific whales. In some cultures there may not be as high an awareness about the misuse of natural resources, and the people may be under the impression that they will not "run out" of whales. How do cultural or ceremonial beliefs affect the balance between whales and humans? How would this problem be solved? These are a sample of the numerous problems students could explore when probing into the delicate balance of coexistence between humans and animals or plants.

BEAUMONT MIDDLE SCHOOL
AND WHAT DO YOU BELIEVE?

Thirty-two students enrolled in a prealgebra class at Beaumont Middle School explored ways to find truth in advertising and uncover hidden messages sent by the press and advertisers. Students also examined different approaches to data organization and presentation, along with the role that statistics and probability play in interpreting data and information. The real-world problem in this unit was centered on accurately interpreting the bombardment of messages sent through television, newspapers, radio, billboards, and other media. Students are targeted by advertisers as customers and potential customers. The marketing industry is highly interested in marketing its products to young adolescents. Through learning how to interpret and differentiate between fact and inferences and through understanding emotional appeal, students discover the hidden and persuasive messages sent in advertising. Students involved in the unit taught by Dayle Spitzer, intern teacher, were sixth, seventh, and eighth graders, representing a wide range of ages within one class.

Beaumont Middle School is located in the Northeast section of Portland. The 720 students make up a student body with approximately 65% Caucasian, 30% African American, and 5% representing other ethnic groups. Of the students, 25% qualify for free or reduced-price lunches. The school was built in 1921, with an additional section added in 1991. Many of the staff have worked at Beaumont for a number of years and are committed to providing a quality education for the students.

The real-world problem-solving unit of interpreting advertising and other media messages was taught over a 6-week period and included several lessons focused on probability and statistics, to align with curriculum expectations. Students had previous experience with graphing and charting and drew on this knowledge when designing their own displays of data.

What Do You Believe?

Unit Overview. Today's youths are bombarded with advertisements and television commercials. Sifting through the inferred statements to find the factual information is an important skill. Students' work revolves around the problem of sorting through advertising and media presentations when gathering and analyzing the information. Students will contrast and compare audio, visual, print, and other forms of advertising and information presentations as they search for "truth in advertising."

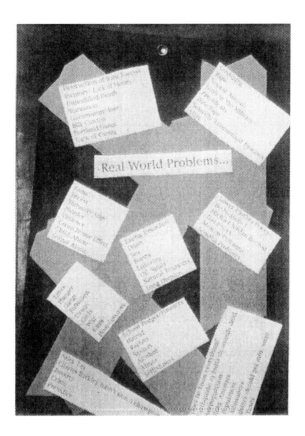

Photo 3.19. Real-World Problems Generated by Dayle's Students

Unit Goals. A major goal for the unit is drawn from the National Curriculum and Evaluation Standards (NCTM, 1989). Standard 10 for the fifth through eighth grade is statistics, which includes the following: collecting, organizing, and describing data; constructing, reading, and interpreting graphs, tables, and charts; making inferences and convincing arguments based on data analysis; evaluating arguments based on data analysis; and developing an appreciation for statistical methods as powerful means for decision making. All of these activities are related to analysis of advertising because they require students to apply statistical skills and knowledge to the real world of media presentations.

Unit Activities.

1. Identify the numerous ways advertising is present in their lives.
2. Examine how data and information are displayed in news-papers, developing a rationale for the purposes of the visual display.
3. Discuss various purposes for displaying data, specifically in chart, table, and graph format.
4. List several differences between factual and inferential pres-entation, as observed on commercials in the medium of television.
5. Present a short skit based on sampling procedures and dis-cuss the need for representative samples in data collection.
6. Create an example that shows how probability and odds play a role in interpreting information.
7. Compare and contrast information presented through audio media, such as radio or telephone, with written or visual displays.
8. Explain the relationship between a targeted audience and the selection of information presentation.
9. Through a communication activity, explore different ways people might interpret the identical presentation of infor-mation.
10. Construct and present a final project that represents collect-ing, organizing, and displaying data.

Lesson #1: How Do You Know if It Is True?

Objective. Students brainstorm different approaches used to pre-sent information to large audiences and the personal effect different advertising or media displays have had on them.

Opening Activity. Hold up the television guide. Ask the students if everything they see on television is true. Discuss their responses.

Lesson Activities

1. Provide a copy of today's newspaper to each group of four students. Ask them to cut out an article or advertisement they

think is "true" and cut out an article or advertisement that is "not true." Each group develops its justification of true or not true information presentations with this activity.

2. Each group presents its selected articles or advertising to the whole class while also discussing their rationale for true or not true articles. The newspaper articles are taped to either the true side of a poster or the not true side.

3. Brainstorm with the class about ways we receive information. Ask students, "How do we know what to believe?" Discuss responses and have each child record the group's list of possible sources of presenting information.

Closing Activity. Looking at the poster of true and not true articles or advertising, write about the ways people come to decide if something they read is true or believable.

Materials
1. Today's issue of the local newspaper
2. Scissors, tape, poster board
3. Paper and pens

Lesson #2: Newspapers and Data

Objective. Students identify the different formats of data presentation as viewed in different sections of the newspaper.

Opening Activity. Ask the students to think of the newspaper and how it is divided into different sections. Ask the students to name as many sections of the paper as they can. Write the sections on the board.

Lesson Activities
1. Give each group a different section of the paper. Ask them to review their section and present a description to the entire class.
2. Have one student from each group come to the front of the room, holding that group's section of the newspaper. Discuss the following questions:

     a. Which section has the most pictures? Why?

     b. Where do you find probability? (Discuss the definition of probability if some students are unclear on the meaning.)

     c. What is on the front page? Why?

     d. Compare how information in the sports section is presented as opposed to information in the living section. What are the differences?

     e. How would the business section look if it did not display numbers?

Closing Activity. Each student talks with his or her partner about the newspaper and something new they learned about the rationale behind the presentation of data.

Materials
1. Copies of the local newspaper

Lesson #3: Why Use Charts, Tables, or Graphs?

Objective. Students interpret data as displayed on a chart, a graph, and a table.

Opening Activity. Each student brings a chart, table, or graph to school. Ask students to work with their small group to describe the information on the data display.

Lesson Activities
1. Discuss the organization of data and different formats for display of data. Using one of the charts, ask the class to organize the same information in a table format and again in a graph format. Discuss the differences and similarities between formats. Ask students to think of a rationale for using one particular format over another.

2. Pull data from several different graphs, writing the data on the board. Ask the students to think of different variables to use as one of the organizers for the display (e g , time, amount, frequency, money, or costs). Ask each small group to develop its own data display, using a chart, table, graph, or other display that can be justified.

Photo 3.20. Table Showing Each Student's Allowance and Class Average

3. Discuss the different formats the students used in their presentation of data.

Closing Activity. Ask the students to look through the newspaper and magazines in the room and cut out three different types of data displays. Each student selects one of the displays to write a justification or explanation of why the statistician selected this particular format.

Materials
1. Newspapers and magazines
2. Scissors, tape, glue

Lesson #4: Facts and Inferences

Objective. Students examine several television commercials and differentiate between facts and inferences.

Opening Activity. Ask students to think about how people spend their time outside of school and work. What do you see on television besides the show? Why are there commercials and what is the intent of commercials and advertising? Write responses on board and discuss student ideas.

Lesson Activities
1. Students watch a videotaped television commercial about a cold medicine. The teacher and students discuss the major point of the commercial and the message presented to the viewers. Students sort the information into the categories of facts, statistics, nonfacts, and inferences. Replay the video several times to record all information.

2. Ask the students to determine how the advertisers obtained the facts and how the facts were displayed. Was the message drawn from direct facts or implied or inferred in the commercial? Ask each group to discuss the decision-making rationale they used to determine if the information was factual or inferential. How do the students differentiate factual from inferential?

3. Watch several more commercials, going through the same process of differentiating between factual and nonfactual information and between implied and statistical data.

Closing Activity. Ask the students to think of their favorite commercial and to write about the reason it is their favorite. Did the commercial sell you on the product? Why or why not?

Materials
1. Videotapes of several current commercials
2. VCR player

Lesson #5: What Is Sampling?

Objective. Students discuss the purpose of sampling and accurate and inaccurate uses of sample populations.

Opening Activity. Ask the students how we could find out the favorite brand potato chip of 11- to 13-year-olds in Portland. Would

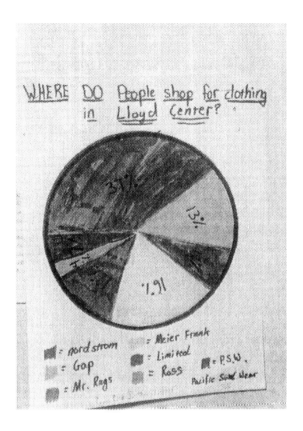

Photo 3.21. Graph Representing Where People Shop at the Local Mall

we have to ask everyone between the ages of 11 and 13? Why or why not? Discuss their ideas and responses.

Lesson Activities
1. Discuss the meaning of the terms *sample, representative sample,* and *random samples* with the class. Provide access to dictionaries and the computer encyclopedia program as needed.
2. Ask the students to think of their favorite candy bar. What would happen if their grandparents were asked what candy bars 11- to 13-year-olds buy most often? Would their grandparents be correct? What would happen if the data were collected about their age group from their grandparents?

Would it be as accurate as information from them? Would the information be accurate if only 10 students were asked to name their favorite candy bar? Why or why not?

3. Brainstorm different ways data could be collected and how polls are conducted, including phone surveys, the Gallup Poll, written surveys, door-to-door surveys or polls, the number of a certain CD purchased that week, and the like. Discuss the different survey methods.

Closing Activity. Students work with a partner and think of information they might want to collect at school. How could they collect this information? Who would they ask? How many people would they survey to obtain helpful information? Partners work together to create a short skit or other activity to represent their survey and results.

Materials
1. Empty (or full) bags of potato chips
2. Candy bar wrappers

Lesson #6: Probability and Odds

Objective. Students compose a probability statement that demonstrates their understanding of probability.

Opening Activity. Holding up a nickel, ask the students what the probability is that the nickel will land with the heads side facing up (50% chance of landing heads up). Discuss how they came to this answer and how they could check the answer.

Lesson Activities
1. Students think of the probability of the nickel landing heads up if the nickel were tossed four times. Discuss the students' responses to the question and have each group test the situation with a nickel, recording its data as the coin is tossed. Share the findings on the board and compile into one table. Discuss results and probability with the class.
2. Ask the class to think of times they have heard of probability. Share their experiences and interpretations of probability.

3. Discuss a recent weather forecast calling for a 60% chance of rain. Does this mean it will rain 60% of the day or that it will most likely rain sometime during the day? How do you know what the probability of rain is for this day? What does probability mean in terms of the weather forecast?

Closing Activity. Students work with a partner to create a probability statement that can be substantiated. Students write their statements and share with the class.

Materials
1. Nickels
2. Recent weather forecast from newspaper

Lesson #7: Listening to Data or Information

Objective. Students compare and contrast information presented through audio means, such as the radio or telephone, with written or visual displays.

Opening Activity. Play a morning announcement recorded from their favorite radio station. Ask the students to separate fact from inference, noting how voice tone, music, volume, and announcer's reaction affect the message. Discuss their responses to the question and to the radio message.

Lesson Activities
1. Students work in small groups with a set of data about a specific product (food) and write a script for two 30-second commercials, one promoting the product and one that downplays the information and presents a negative view of the product, although using the same information for both commercials.
2. Each group records its commercial, listens to the recording, and makes any adjustments before the final production.
3. Groups present their recordings and ask the listeners to rate the product based on the commercial. Students analyze the data to determine if their presentations affected the selling of the product through the commercial.

Photo 3.22. Dayle Listens to Students as They Develop a Commercial

Closing Activity. Ask students to think of three ways an announcer or advertiser can affect the image of their product on a radio announcement. Share and discuss their ideas.

Materials
1. Recording of morning announcement from students' favorite radio station
2. Tape player

Lesson #8: The Audience

Objective. Students explain the relationship between the advertising or information presentation and the intended audience.

Opening Activity. Watch two commercials for toys. One commercial raves about low prices and the quality of the toy. The other commercial shows children having a great time with the toy. In small groups, ask the students to identify similarities and differences between the commercials. (Although you do not mention *intended audience,* see if this term arises in the student conversations.)

Lesson Activities
1. Students think of reasons why the information was presented differently (or different information presented about similar toys).
2. Discuss the meaning of audience through the following questions. When are the students an audience? What does it mean to be an audience? Thinking of a previous lesson, is their parent an audience for the same radio station as they are? Who decides an audience is an audience? What would happen if an advertiser missed the intended audience?
3. Thinking of the lessons on probability, ask students to devise a short story that links audience with probability and information presentation.

Closing Activity. Students share the draft of their short story with a partner and help edit the writing.

Materials
1. Videotapes of two toy commercials geared for different audiences
2. VCR player

Lesson #9: Different Is Different

Objective. Students dramatize different interpretations of the same message.

Opening Activity. Play a tape recording of rattling noises and the sound of breaking glass. Ask students to draw a picture of the incident that they "overheard."

Lesson Activities
1. Students work in their groups to discuss their interpretations of the incident. Identify and explain similarities and differences.
2. Students listen to a recording of statistics from a recent ball game, drawing a picture of what they heard on the tape. Again, students work in small groups and share their interpretations.

3. In which instance was there more agreement among students? Discuss bias and clarity in presenting data. What reduces bias?

4. Read examples from the newspaper that demonstrate unintentional bias, use of only supportive data, Hawthorne effect (see Homans, 1965), and poor data collection. Discuss the impact each of these examples of bias has on the interpretation of the information.

Closing Activity. Working in pairs, students select a picture from a magazine or a newspaper article and develop two statements or interpretations that describe the article or picture in two different ways. Students write each statement on an index card and attach to the picture or article.

Materials
1. Tape recording of sounds of rattling and breaking glass
2. Tape recording of statistics from recent ball game
3. Tape player
4. Magazines and newspapers
5. Scissors
6. Index cards
7. Stapler

Lesson #10: Look At What We Learned!

Objective. Pairs of students identify a problem, survey an audience, organize data, and present information through a visual display.

Opening Activity. Students think of information they might like to find out about advertising, products, other students, and so on. Discuss possible ideas with the class.

Lesson Activities
1. Pairs of students identify a problem to research and begin outlining steps to obtain information or data through a survey.
2. Each pair develops a written or visual proposal of its research project.

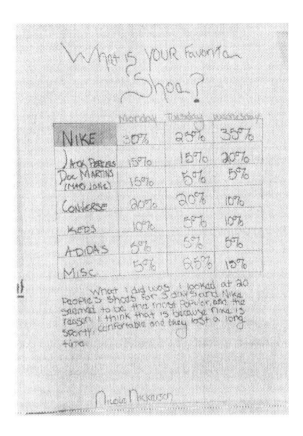

Photo 3.23. Survey and Table Representing Favorite Shoes

3. Conference individually with all pairs and provide resources or assistance as needed to help them begin the project.

4. Throughout the 2-week period when students are gathering data as they conduct their survey, set aside several class periods or portions of class to work on organizing the data. Provide time for students to work at the computers and store and manipulate their data in a statistic program.

5. Review the different graphs, charts, and tables. Encourage students to think of several ways that their data could be displayed.

6. Students organize a presentation night, when parents and neighbors are invited to school to listen to students present their projects. Each pair will develop a poster table, with tables, graphs, or charts and other visuals supporting its research. Guests will walk through the area and listen to the student presentations.

Closing Activity. Students write an essay or develop a presentation describing their research and the relationship between the data, the way the data was presented, and the message the students wanted their audience to receive.

Materials
1. Chart paper, poster paper, pens

Unit Resources

Literature (Fiction and Nonfiction)

Avi. (1991). *Nothing but the Truth.* New York: Orchard Books.
Bright, G., Harvey, J., & Wheeler, M. (1981). Fair Games, Unfair Games. In Albert Schulte (Ed.), *Teaching Statistics and Probability.* Reston, VA: NCTM.
Evans, C. R. (1994). *Marketing Channels: Infomercials and the Future of Televised Marketing.* Englewood Cliffs, NJ: Prentice Hall.
Liston, R. A. (1977). *Why We Think As We Do.* New York: Franklin Watts.
Mathematics Resource Project. (1978). *Statistics and Informational Organization.* Palo Alto, CA: Creative Publications.
O'Sullivan, C. (1990). *Television: Identifying Propaganda Techniques.* San Diego, CA: Greenhaven.
Seiden, H. (1990). *Advertising Pure and Simple.* New York: AMACOM.
Steffems, B., & Buggy, J. (1992). *Free Speech: Identifying Propaganda Techniques.* San Diego, CA: Greenhaven.

Teacher Resources

Wurman, R. (1989). *Information Anxiety.* New York: Bantam Books.

Summary of What Do You Believe?

Students were amazed to find that many of the commercials they had listened to or read presented information that might be misleading. How many times have you read an ad about losing 30 pounds in 20 days? This type of advertisement runs almost weekly in most newspapers yet might refer to one person out of many who use the product advertised in the commercial. The students became much more critical in their analysis of data and messages presented through the media.

By designing their own research project, conducting surveys, organizing data, and presenting the information in the display format of their choice, students became aware of the variety of manipulations to data or information that could shape the message to the audience. Many students remembered purchasing a toy they had seen on television and "had to own." They remembered quite vividly the feeling of disappointment with the real thing when they finally played with the toy: It looked so much better on television than out of the package.

This unit was taught in a math class and provides an example of an integrative teaching and learning unit taught in a single-discipline setting. Students were completing goals in mathematics (graphing, charting, interpreting statistics, and probability) while also using communication skills (writing, conducting surveys, and presenting their research project), exploring social studies (effect of age, gender, and other characteristics on purchasing and other decisions), science (collecting data and drawing inferences and results from data), and fine arts (using music and art as influences in advertising). In the words of one student, "I like working like this rather than the textbook. Hands-on is way better, you remember more. I think projects like this build responsibility and prepare [you] for the rest of your life."

Related topics that might lead to problem solving for other groups of students include exploring bias in the written media, using surveys and data in decision making in the corporate world and in government, and examining a variety of influences on people that are less obvious, such as color, sound, smell, and other sensory input. As children make sense of their world, they become tremendously curious about influences and fairness. Bias, propaganda, statistics, and probability are important areas that lend themselves to becoming the focus of problem solving.

Photo 3.24. Graph Representing People's Favorite Time to Take Vacations

SUMMARY OF CASE EXAMPLES OF INTEGRATIVE TEACHING AND LEARNING THROUGH REAL-WORLD PROBLEM SOLVING

Each of these real-world problem-solving units or case studies acquired a unique approach to teaching and learning as the problem solving progressed. As we visited Nalani and her students, we found them actively seeking information about their front yard and learning the value of wetlands and the essential contributions of a wetland region as they made decisions about the land use of their front yard. Susan and her students looked at an everyday object, shoes, and entered a search for knowledge about resources used in shoe manufacturing, the difference between renewable and nonrenewable resources, and how purchases affect our environment. The students in Kim's class were concerned about the decreasing number of salmon and became aware of different stakeholders' interest in salmon and the relationship between humans and salmon. Students in the math class moved far beyond the traditional math textbook or worksheet

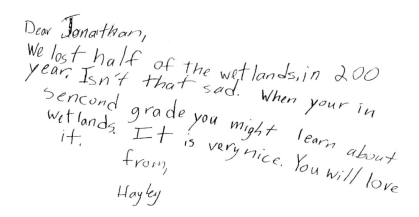

Figure 3.8. Letter Written by Second Grader to Younger Brother About Wetlands

lessons (as noted by many students in their positive evaluation of the unit). This age group is strongly influenced by the media and was amazed at the hidden agenda in many of the commercials they had listened to or seen many times. Their exploration through their own marketing and survey research enabled them to develop individual interests and share interesting new findings with the class.

The students' interests and drive to obtain new information relevant to solving their specific problem allowed them to direct the focus of each of these units as it unfolded. During the process of the actual unit, each teacher gradually became more comfortable with taking cues from students and facilitating students as they searched for solutions to problems that they considered important. The case examples presented in this section are comprehensive in order to share the large picture of the entire problem-solving unit. Other teachers might need less extensive plans to accomplish a similar teaching and learning unit focused on problem solving.

The results of integrative teaching and learning through real-world problem solving find students who are eager to delve into learning activities, because they feel empowered to impact their community with the solution from their problem solving. For instance, Nalani's second graders are adamant about preserving their wetlands. Several parents and community members had requested that the wetlands area be mowed and trimmed to improve the landscaping of the school. No way, according to these students. The students held a forum with several administrators and teachers, introducing their wetland and the need to maintain the wetland in its natural state. Their individual views of the wetland were video-taped, and each student received a tape to take home and share with his or her family. The feedback was overwhelming. Parents were surprised that 7-year-olds would understand wetlands and the environment to the extent that this group of students demonstrated. Support for retention of the wetlands in its current state has increased significantly. These students know they have made an impact in their community and are empowered to continue their work.

Students in each of these classrooms have a different success story to tell about their experiences with real-world problem solving. The fifth-grade students in Susan's class were amazed at the different materials used in manufacturing shoes and that their purchases have an impact on the environment. Although they were familiar with recycling programs, they had not thought about the relationship between purchasing an item and the effect this may have on the environment. Kim's class became so interested in the concept and applications of problem solving, several students chose to work on all assignments in a problem-solving format following the salmon and human coexistence unit. Dayle's students wrote about the importance of learning about truth (and nontruth) in advertising and actually tested their knowledge by developing their own survey and presenting it to the parents. When each of the classrooms discussed in this chapter was visited, new and unique activities and learning processes were observed. Each unit was similar in the sense that an integrative approach to teaching and learning allowed students to create new understandings and extend and expand prior knowledge in multiple disciplines as they moved through a meaningful problem-solving process.

Notes

1. These aquatic resource education materials were developed in part with funding from the U.S. Fish and Wildlife Service. Permission to reprint lesson adapted from these materials was provided by the U.S. Fish and Wildlife Service.

2. Portions of this lesson and several others are adapted from activities in *Salmonids in the Classroom* (BCTF Lesson Aids Service, 100-550 West 6th Avenue, Vancouver, B.C., Canada V524P2) and from *Water, Water Everywhere* . . . (Oregon Fish and Wildlife).

3. This lesson is adapted from an activity in *Salmonids in the Classroom* (BCTF Lesson Aids Service, 100-550 West 6th Avenue, Vancouver, B.C., Canada V524P2) and from *Water, Water Everywhere* . . . (Oregon Fish and Wildlife).

4

Assessing Integrative Learning

Authentic assessment, like learning, occurs most naturally and lastingly when it is in a meaningful context and when it relates to authentic concerns and problems faced by students.

—Brooks and Brooks
(1993, p. 96)

The terms *evaluation* and *assessment* are used by educators to indicate measurement of student learning. Typically, evaluation refers to a judgment about student knowledge, student behavior, attitude, or performance, and assessment is a strategy used to gather data (often continuously) about student learning (Freiberg & Driscoll, 1992). The results may be used for assigning a grade, for developing a profile or indicator of student knowledge or learning, for making instructional changes or modifications to facilitate student learning, or for communication about student learning. There are multiple purposes of assessment and a wide array of assessment formats or strategies to use when looking at student learning.

In integrative teaching and learning, students guide their work toward problem solving, and assessment is most appropriate when conducted in stages of diagnostic (pre) measure, formative (assessing learning during the activities), and summative (following completion of the unit) formats. Later in this chapter, examples of assessment from the real-world problem examples will be presented, along with discussion about the impact of assessment on unit planning, lesson activities, and future teaching and curriculum decisions.

Importance of Assessment

Evaluation and assessment in education have become increasingly important as our nation's performance in schooling is reviewed. Reform measures abound since the publication of *A Nation at Risk* by the National Commission on Excellence in Education in 1983. Two frequent themes repeatedly found in reform reports are to increase educational standards and to improve means to measure these standards. At the national, state, and local levels, educators are currently examining educational outcomes while remaining cognizant of the many annual reports based on standardized test results published for national and international comparisons.

Unfortunately, a mismatch between the educational outcomes or curriculum of a school and the content of standardized tests is the norm more often than not. Does this mean that a teacher should alter the school curriculum and essentially teach to the standardized test? Or should alternative assessments be developed and used to match the educational goals or outcomes for the school and district? These are critical questions that are asked by teachers as test results become public information, to the point of test scores being published in local newspapers along with specific grade level and school site information. If authentic assessment measures are developed at the state or local level, concerns are also raised about the quality of these assessment practices and the background training that educators have received in assessment literacy (Stiggins, 1991). Some of the mystique and confusion surrounding assessment must be lessened to allow teachers and students to develop ways to examine their learning and make decisions about current and future learning based on the assessment data collected throughout the learning process.

Teaching and Assessment

Clear connections should exist between teaching and assessment, particularly when teaching and learning are viewed in the constructivist sense, with students creating meaning and understanding from their learning. Following this line of thought, the assessment process itself would derive from student learning and input and serve as a tool to demonstrate the knowledge, concepts, and skills the student has developed. Curriculum, teaching, learning, and assessment would be in alignment.

General expectations or learning outcomes would be clearly articulated at the onset of the unit, with input from students in developing criteria for determining success in learning. By developing and communicating the expected outcomes at the beginning of the unit, students have outlined expectations to follow as they move through problem solving and develop their final project in their real-world problem-solving unit. Teaching, learning, and assessment have become integrated, following the thinking of Grant Wiggins (1992), who states that "good teaching is inseparable from good assessing" (p. 33).

Purpose of Assessment

Several purposes of assessment are to obtain and provide information about student learning, to diagnose student knowledge prior to a unit of study, to identify student interests, to provide instructional feedback and indication of necessary instructional modifications if students are not learning the material, and to determine student learning gains as compared to preassessment measures prior to a unit of study. This list is by no means exhaustive but is meant to stimulate teachers' thinking about the potential of assessment in terms of student learning in integrative teaching and learning.

Communication

Another important use of assessment is for communication about student learning. This communication may occur between students and parents, between students, between teachers and students, and between community members (the public) and students. Authentic assessment connected to learning provides a language to use in communicating about student learning.

Students of all ages are interested in obtaining feedback about their own learning and completed work. Conferences, written comments, and shared conversations in the class are examples of formats that provide descriptive feedback to a student. This format of information provides far more feedback than a letter grade on a paper or test. Using authentic or performance-based assessment throughout the integrative teaching and learning unit helps students check on their individual progress and note their learning gains as they proceed through the problem-solving process. Setting benchmarks together as a class or as individuals for marking progress through the unit enables students to gain feedback on a regular basis, prior to completion of the entire project.

Parents, community members, other students, and school personnel are additional important audiences interested in assessment of student learning. Frequent feedback about student learning to parents is essential. Developing formats beyond a report card provide deeper and more meaningful ways to relate student learning to parents. Several examples of formats found to be successful in communicating with parents will be described later in this chapter.

When reaching solutions or gaining information pertinent to the real-world problem, students were eager to provide important information to share with other students in the school and their community members. Students communicated findings to the community through presentations and displays for staff and students at the school, community presentations, meetings, and letters to family members. Looking at assessment of learning through the perspective of authentic assessment of meaningful learning shifted the emphasis from a grade or score to a portrayal of the actual knowledge and skills gained from the student's participation in an integrated unit of study.

Assessment Formats

Traditional standardized tests tend to structure the content of the test around basic skills expected to be mastered by students at a particular age or grade level. By comparison, authentic assessment asks students to demonstrate or exhibit their learning through application (Brooks & Brooks, 1993). In many cases, students do not stop their work on problem solving to "take" a test, they simply compile portions of their research and update an observer on their findings and the process they were using to approach the problem. Learning is not interrupted for test taking, because the teacher's role is to observe and discuss learning and the learning process with students as they are engaged in their work.

A major distinction between authentic assessment and perform-ance assessment is found when examining the various types of performance assessments. Authentic assessment requires the per-formance of an activity in a meaningful context, thus the assessment is considered to be authentic to the learning and the learner. Carol Meyer (1992) refers to authentic assessment occurring when the student completes or demonstrates a task or behavior in a "real-life context" (p. 40). Performance assessment requires students to dem-onstrate their knowledge or skills, allowing the teacher and student to observe both the learning and the process by which the learning was demonstrated (Rudner & Boston, 1994). In this chapter the term *authentic assessment* will be used to illustrate the activity of gathering evidence of student learning within a meaningful context. It is im-portant to note that both the teacher and the student are engaged in gathering assessment information.

Authentic assessment requires a close examination of teaching, learning, and assessment. Teachers and students work together to develop criteria for determining satisfactory performance or demon-strations of learning, which also impact the content and process of the curriculum. Because the criteria are developed at the beginning of the unit, benchmarks are visited throughout the unit, and revisions to earlier curriculum and assessment goals may need to occur to meet the changes implicit in constructivist classrooms. Students are clearly aware of the direction they are heading with their work, because they were involved in developing the curriculum and assessment criteria. Authentic assessment also provides students with a vehicle for show-ing how they learned or reached answers and moves the focus away from one correct answer for all students toward a demonstration or display of knowledge within the context of the learning situation.

Authentic Assessment Formats

Portfolios

There are multiple formats of authentic assessment in use in our classrooms. Educators are developing and experimenting with dif-ferent techniques to assess student learning at the classroom level. One of the more common assessment formats is the portfolio. A portfolio can refer to "anything from cumulative student writing folders to elaborate personal scrapbooks" (Sunstein, 1992, p. xi). Artists, models, and architects have developed portfolios as part of their profession for many years. The introduction of portfolios in education is fairly recent, with many teachers finding portfolios helpful in creating a portrayal of student work and learning.

Portfolios typically refer to a folder that contains representations of student work. In most classes, students are involved in the selection process for their portfolios and choose examples of their work that represent criteria developed by the teacher and the students. For example, students might decide to place the first essay written in the school year, including their rough draft and several revisions, in their portfolios to represent their work at the beginning of the year. The students might also reflect on their work, adding comments about strengths and suggestions for improving their essays. Teacher comments are also included with the student work. As the year progresses, students continue to add to their portfolios, again reflecting on their work and learning. The portfolio should "furnish a broad portrait of individual performance, assembled over time" (Rudner & Boston, 1994, p. 3).

Portfolios are applicable to all subject areas and grade levels and reflect authentic learning, which "is evident when learners participate in high-quality, meaningful activity and generate documents reflecting their thinking and learning" (Henning-Stout, 1994, p. 49). In mathematics, students might select examples of problems that required work over a period of time and represent their best efforts. A social studies portfolio might contain maps, reports, drawings, and portions of projects completed by students. Photographs, videotapes, drawings, tape recordings, written work, and letters might be in a portfolio. Portfolios also provide an opportunity for students to see the connection between subject areas; for example, a written explanation of a science experiment could require writing, mathematics, and an understanding of a science concept. In integrative teaching and learning through real-world problem solving, portfolios become a tool for documenting the problem-solving process and keeping track of the learning as students solve the problem.

Several states have adopted portfolios for statewide assessment, with student portfolios moving to different grade levels with the student. Two common concerns teachers raise about portfolios are management of the portfolio (e.g., where to keep the portfolio, how to share papers and projects with the student's family and still keep the portfolio content at school, how to store large pieces of work) and how to decide what should be kept in a portfolio over a period of years. These types of decisions require thoughtful consideration by students and school personnel, because the portfolio will travel with the student from elementary school to middle school to the high school and, potentially, to the workplace or higher education if students and school districts find the portfolio to be an accurate and valid representation of the students and their work.

Demonstrations and Performances

Showing what you know through a performance or demonstration allows students to display their knowledge and learning in an active exhibit. A demonstration or performance might be developed by a small group, the whole class, or a single student. A demonstration might be as simple as having a student read a passage from a novel and use prior knowledge of the story and characters to interpret the meaning of the passage in a conversation with other students. A more complex demonstration might require students to perform several steps with an open-ended situation. For example, a group of students might be asked to determine and justify the best travel route from Philadelphia to Los Angeles. Their presentation would include alternative routes and consider factors such as travel time, costs, scenery, student interest in certain cities or states (relatives, places, events, etc.), and their route of choice, including the rationale for selecting and traveling this route. Students explore mathematics, language arts, social studies, and geography to reach a solution for their demonstration. While observing the demonstration, a teacher would be able to determine student understanding of the original problem and problem-solving skills used to reach a solution. Students would access many disciplines as needed throughout their demonstration, which would expose the problem-solving process used throughout the project.

Demonstrations and presentations also require communication skills, which are necessary for success in the workforce of today and the future. Students learn to organize information and present their views and facts in an interesting format for an audience. The teacher and students could develop a rubric or criteria scale for the presentation that would reflect both the content of the presentation and the format or skill of presenting. Students would know in advance what the expectations for the presentation were and respond by preparing for the demonstration according to the established criteria.

Experiments and Investigations

Several science educators have created an assessment procedure in alignment with good science teaching (Shavelson & Baxter, 1992). Instead of testing student knowledge of science through recall of a list of science vocabulary words, these teachers are asking students to conduct investigations in the presence of a judge (science teacher or scientist). These investigations meet the criteria of authentic assessment, because students are expected to demonstrate and continue their learning in a meaningful context.

Student work is assessed on the process of performing the investigation as well as the outcome or results of the investigation. Observation of a student's experiment can provide assessment of the student's understanding of a concept, the student's ability to carry out a scientific process, and the student's ability to apply facts and concepts. Again, several disciplines are used during the investigation. Students read instructions, record results, analyze findings, draw conclusions, and contrast and compare results with prior knowledge. When investigations and experiments are posed as assessment measures and relate to classroom instruction and activities, students continue to learn as they apply skills, concepts, and prior knowledge in a new situation.

Visual Representations

In certain learning situations, depiction of prior knowledge and knowledge gained after involvement in a unit can best be displayed through a visual representation. For instance, students are about to embark on a study of the problem of what to bring with them on a trip to the moon. Prior to the unit, each student draws a picture portraying five essential items he or she would take along to the moon. An essay might accompany the drawing, with a justification included for each item. At the conclusion of the unit, the students would again draw five essential items to pack for their journey to the moon. The two drawings could be compared and contrasted, with students explaining the difference between the drawings and the reasons for changing items they would select.

Another approach with visual representations would be to begin a mural with the class at the beginning of a unit and continue to add to the mural as the students gain more knowledge. When studying about water quality, students might begin a mural with pictures of water-saving techniques of which they are aware and continue to add to the mural throughout the unit. The mural might include numbers (amount of water units saved), words (descriptions of water-saving procedures), social studies (how other cultures save water), and artwork (visual portrayal of water usage in our lives).

Essays and Journals

Teachers have turned to written work as an assessment tool in the form of essays for many years. During the past decade, writing has been viewed more as a process than a finished product, as teachers encouraged students to create outlines and drafts of their writing in the beginning stages of developing an idea.

In integrative teaching and learning, use of a journal for recording thoughts, ideas, findings, and feelings about the problem-solving process is an effective technique for assessment in the formative and summative sense. Students record information and thoughts on a regular basis and can review their work from earlier times and form their own assessments of personal learning and growth. Sharing ideas through a journal can create a dialogue between the teacher and a student on an individual level, providing feedback and sharing thoughts through the problem-solving process. Some students may prefer written communication to verbal communication and share more of their knowledge and learnings in a journal or essay format. Much is learned from writing down thoughts and rereading them later (Voss, 1992). When classroom time is set aside on a regular basis for reflection, with writing viewed as a tool for thinking and learning, students have the opportunity to create meaning for their work on real-world problem setting within an authentic context, thus writing can be added to the list of authentic assessment measures.

Creation of a Product

Group or individual projects often lead to the development of a product that can be displayed as the culmination of the project. Again, the students and teacher work together to develop criteria for determining the success of a product at the beginning of the unit of study. A rubric representing a 5-point scale, with criteria established for each point of the scale, could clearly articulate the expectations for the product.

Students involved in studying the problem of earthquakes and designing buildings to be "earthquake proof" could build a model house that incorporated the safety features that they determined were important, based on their research of this real-world problem. As in many real-world problems, information must be gathered from experts in the field, either through phone calls, letters, visits, or via electronic mail systems, to gain the most current information and facts. Students might talk to county planners, architects, and geologists as they develop plans for their model building. Knowledge of appropriate materials and structural requirements would be necessary to demonstrate a grasp of problem-solving knowledge in the earthquake example. Students would have explored the real-world problem of earthquakes through the disciplines of mathematics (development of a scale of the model), social studies (buildings and homes), science (study of earthquakes), art (construction of a visual model), and communication (contacting experts and conducting research). The final product, the model of a "safe" earthquake building, would serve as an assessment of student learning and application of knowledge.

Multimedia Technology

Computers, camcorders, CD-ROM drives, optical drives, scanners, and laser printers are fast becoming the technology of the classroom. Students are embracing these new forms of technology and, in many cases, helping their teachers learn how to use them. These tools provide another format for recording learning activities for use in authentic assessment, as well as providing a system for storing recorded events.

Teachers and students are finding the camcorder to be helpful in recording the development of a project or major unit, as well as recording the outcomes. Often, students are reluctant to leave portfolios, essays, pictures, and other work at school. Recording this work with the camcorder onto a videotape allows a record of the work to be stored at school and the actual work to go home with the student. Parents may "borrow" the videotape and review their child's learning on a regular basis. The videotaping may continue over a period of several years, with both the students and the teachers deciding when or what should be recorded. The videotape can then be transferred to a laser disk for storage. The laser disk accommodates large amounts of data yet is small enough to fit into a student's folder.

Viewing the learning process and progress of a student through a visual record, such as the videotape, provides a comprehensive picture of student learning. Multimedia technology adds many more dimensions beyond the traditional format of a paper-and-pencil test when we now view students collaborating on a project, discussing ideas, organizing events, and planning and producing a final product. The use of multimedia techniques for assessing learning meshes nicely with integrative teaching and learning, as the technology provides a view of students working in their milieu as they move through the problem-solving process and create solutions to real-world problems.

Group Forum and Town Hall Meeting

The forum or town hall meeting format consists of students presenting findings to community members, with students leading the conversation as the "experts" on the problem or issue. Conversations include questions and answers and require students to justify their findings and conclusions. The forum allows observers to note student learning in the realm of real-world problem solving and at a level using higher-level thinking skills. Students evaluate their work and the work of others in the field of the real-world problem to reach a possible solution to the problem.

As in the other formats of authentic assessment, students are working within a meaningful context and continue their learning when engaged in the forum or town hall meeting. Questions arise that may bring new information or insights into the picture, and students will have opportunities to rethink prior perceptions of the problem and of the solution. Disciplines or subject areas are integrated as questions and answers move across disciplines. Real-world problems and potential solutions tend to raise controversy, and students find themselves in the role of providing answers and possible solutions to important problems that are of concern to the community.

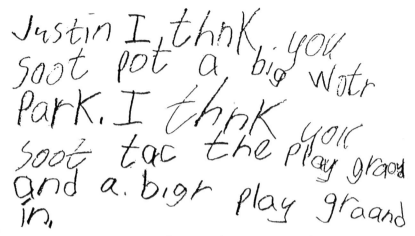

Figure 4.1. Student Journal Entry About Water Park
NOTE: "I think you should put a big water park. I think you should take the playground and a bigger playground in." By Justin. (This was written *prior* to studying the front yard in response to the question: "What should we do with the front yard of the school?")

Assessment Samples From
Integrative Teaching and Learning Units

Samples of assessment formats used in each of the four integrative units presented in Chapter 3 will be discussed and described in this section. Each teacher developed assessment procedures to demonstrate learning gained over the period of the work on real-world problem solving, as well as being appropriate for the age and interests of their students.

Our Front Yard

Nalani's second graders began their real-world problem unit by drawing a picture of the front yard of the school as it appeared and a picture of how they would like it to look. They all wrote in their journals about their suggested uses for the front yard of the school. Nalani purposely avoided mention of the terms *wetlands* or *environment* in the beginning of the unit, wanting the students to come to these terms as they gained knowledge about land usage. Several students suggested commercial development of the front yard, including a water park or a Toys "R" Us store. Assessment continued throughout the unit, as students regularly wrote their thoughts and

Dear Mom and Dad,

We are studying about wetlands. Sometimes we go to the front yard and write in our green jernal. In our green jernal we write about wetlands and talk about the swamp. We even make movies. It is so excitinng! Mrs. wineman made a model of our school. We got to see and smell the swamp. We put some water in the school model so we can see if it would go all the way to the bottom. And it did. The first time we were going outside to the front yard evrybody was excited.

Love,
Nadia

Figure 4.2. Letter From Second Grader Near End of Wetland Unit

new learnings in their journals. Nalani responded to the student journals in writing on a weekly basis.

Near the end of the unit, she had a conference with each student about his or her original idea for the front yard and his or her current thinking about the land usage. Each student was excited about the little patch of wetland and how important it is to leave the land alone and preserve its natural state. Students were able to describe the impact of the wetland and the importance it served in their community.

Nalani found that journal writing, conferences, and the final presentation to the community of the video the class developed about the "Our Front Yard" unit served as authentic assessment tools for this unit. She was able to determine student learning by analyzing development of ideas for the land usage prior to the unit, to ideas at the end of the unit. Developing a rubric system to rate student knowledge of environmental impact of wetlands for the preassessment and the postassessment provided a numerical scale for measuring learning. Assessment and learning extended beyond the unit time period, as students continued discussions and their protectiveness toward preserving the wetlands throughout the entire school year.

Choosing Shoes

Susan analyzed the major content areas of the unit and developed a seven question preassessment administered the first day of the unit. Questions were open-ended and students were told that the purpose of the preassessment was to help them let Susan find out what they already knew about the problem of choosing shoes. Each question was assigned a point value of 1, and students received credit for their answers if they were able to provide an answer to the question. Scores on the preassessment ranged from three to seven. Responses also provided direction for Susan, as she found all students were able to give three reasons for wearing shoes, thus eliminating a need to spend time on this section of the unit.

Several activities throughout the unit were useful assessment tools. Students wrote a story from a shoe's perspective, which provided an insight into their writing skills and knowledge of the many functions of shoes. A social studies lesson focused on patents and, as each student developed a new shoe and a patent to go with the shoe, Susan was able to assess their understanding of the patent process and the use of resources in shoe production.

The final project, a small-group presentation about choosing shoes, was to incorporate four of the seven points raised on the preassessment. Susan and the students assessed the projects using a 4-point scale, one point assigned for each of the required components. For example, students were to discuss resources used in making shoes and the impact that this has on the environment. When this topic was covered in the project or presentation, a point was added to the score. Students developed the scoring sheet for their project and were involved in assessing their work, thereby becoming active participants in both curriculum building and in the assessment of the learning.

Each assessment procedure occurred during the flow of the class and was part of the teaching and learning on choosing shoes. Students were assessed based on criteria that they had developed with the teacher and were aware of prior to the assessment.

Salmon and Humans

Kim asked the fifth graders to write what they knew about salmon and what they would like to learn about salmon in a preassessment essay. She recorded their responses to the first part of the question to use as a comparison with the postassessment essay.

Figure 4.3. Drawing Depicting Ship Transporting Rubber to Shoe Factories

117

Photo 4.1. Student-Made Chart Outlining Learning About Salmon

Several students were aware that salmon spawn and die after laying eggs. They also mentioned that salmon return to the stream or river where they were born. Kim was able to build on this knowledge and knew these students would be able to contribute to discussions about the life cycle of salmon, which was an integral part of the unit.

Kim also observed students as they applied knowledge gained through the unit when they completed assignments such as writing articles for the class newspaper. She recorded her observations on a sheet of paper she carried on a clipboard and was able to keep a written anecdotal record of individual student learning over a period of several months.

Small groups of students worked together to design murals representing the life cycle of the salmon. The murals provided a visual assessment of student understanding of the salmon life cycle and contributed to the assessment profile of each student. The final project, the class newspaper, also provided a written avenue for students to demonstrate their understanding of the issues between salmon survival and humans' impact on the salmon. The postassessment asked students to list characteristics of salmon, describe the life cycle of salmon, and discuss the issue of the declining salmon population, including suggestions for solving this situation. Although the first two questions asked for information at the recall or basic understanding level, the final question was an opportunity for students to share their perception of the salmon and human problem and pose solutions to this problem. Students were required to reflect on the integrative teaching and learning unit, evaluate the situation of salmon and human coexistence, and develop proposals that could potentially benefit salmon and humans.

At the end of the unit, Kim had an individual conference with each student, sharing his or her response to the preassessment and to the postassessment questions. Students were asked to share their views of what they had learned and gained from the unit. These comments were recorded on the postassessment conference page. Through the use of written questions, group projects, and posing the real-world problem as a question on the postassessment, Kim was able to gather data about student learning and share these findings with the students and their parents.

Truth in Advertising

The sixth, seventh, and eighth graders involved in the problem solving regarding truth in advertising (which led to research on consumerism and probability and statistics) began this unit by completing a preassessment, which asked students to give examples of probability, interpret graphs, and describe their favorite commercial. Dayle then asked students to watch five commercials on television and discuss interpretations of data according to statistics presented in commercials. As students spent time analyzing commercials and advertisements, they began to detect the hidden truths and agendas within the advertisements. After watching videos of several popular commercials, students were eager to continue uncovering the facts and messages in the advertising. Students kept a log of television and newspaper advertisements over a 2-week period, noting the intended message and the possible misrepresentation of data. Students shared their logs in small groups several times each week.

The final project and the major assignment in this unit was to develop a survey and complete a research study about a product,

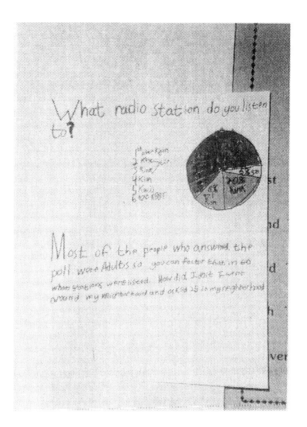

Photo 4.2. Chart Representing Survey Taken to Determine Radio Stations People Choose

object, or any student-selected choice of topic, using statistics and interpretation of data to show the results of the survey. Students spent time developing standards and expectations for a successful project and created their own scoring system or rubric to allocate points for meeting expectations for different components of the project and presentation of the project. Again, assessment was ongoing and part of the learning, with students guiding their learning and the assessment of their learning throughout the construction of their research project.

The real-world problem-solving unit was successful in creating a "problem" from the beginning. The students were active and interested in each trip or lesson and their growth was exciting to watch. My role was the facilitator of the initial problem awareness, and the students carried on with the problem formation and problem solving.

Figure 4.4. Intern's Reflective Notes

Assessment of Teaching or Self-Assessment

Each teacher was also asked to assess her teaching of the integrative unit, both on a daily basis and at the end of the unit. Daily notes tended to discuss which activities were successful and which activities needed modification or improvements. A familiar statement was, "I needed to spend more time helping them accomplish one part of the lesson instead of spending time trying to move through so much material." As they became more familiar with the real-world problem-solving unit, the teachers also became more comfortable with allowing students to move in their own directions and helping them locate resources to answer their questions.

The teachers were unanimous about finding tremendous value in the integrative teaching and learning approach. The final project or culminating activity was seen as an important part of the learning process and a way to enable students to contribute a meaningful product to an important real-world problem. Each teacher also kept notes or a journal throughout the unit and looked back on these notes as she reflected on the unit. More discussion of their recommendations will follow in Chapters 5 and 6.

Summary

Assessing learning in an integrative teaching and learning unit is part of the teaching and learning process. Assessment occurs on a regular basis and is viewed as an important feedback process for students, teachers, and others. Authentic assessment asks students to demonstrate their knowledge and skills in a meaningful setting or activity, which is in alignment with real-world problem solving. Creating open-ended assessment activities with clear connections to the unit goals and objectives and asking students to be involved in creating expectations and criteria for learning establish a classroom environment conducive to success. With integrative teaching and learning, students are able to apply their knowledge across discipline boundaries as they develop solutions to real-world problems, with assessment also integrated within the unit.

5

Looking Back

WHAT WE HAVE LEARNED

I learned so much about being flexible and about coping with issues that were out of my control (such as 598 of the 600 salmon eggs dying before hatching). I also learned a lot about teaching from my students.

—Kim Bauer, fifth-grade teacher

Ownership of Learning

All four of the teachers who developed and taught the units described in Chapter 3 noted the tremendous impact of student ownership of learning when students became immersed in solving their real-world problem. The units were taught after the first quarter of the school year, so teachers had observed student learning and behavior during prior lessons and units. When the real-world problem-solving units were introduced, dramatic changes occurred in all four of these classrooms. Student conversations about different portions of the problem were overheard throughout the day, including lunchtime and recess. Students brought resources and additional information from home, and parents commented on the real-world problems, adding their suggestions and ideas. The teachers attributed the strong student interest in the units to ownership of the learning, in contrast to teacher-directed learning activities, which typically limited the subject or topic to one discipline area and to a scheduled time period. In a real-world problem-solving unit, learning crosses disciplines according to student needs to access information or pull from prior knowledge. The active learning observed by the teachers provided an opportunity for students to use previously learned knowledge and skills as they gained new knowledge in their problem-solving process.

Ownership of learning became a discussion topic in Kim's classroom when students wanted to assume more of the responsibility for monitoring the aquarium temperature and making adjustments as needed. Students involved in the shoe unit discussed their productivity rates when making baby shoes and were amazed to see the rate increase over a 5-day period. These students developed their own method to measure productivity and to monitor shoes made per time unit. In Nalani's second-grade class, students most definitely became gatekeepers of the wetlands area in their attempt to educate the community on the importance of preserving that area. Students in Dayle's class created their own research projects around a self-selected area of interest and taught each other how to screen implied messages when looking for the truth. These projects were owned by the students and viewed by them as their responsibility. We learned from these students the importance of stepping aside as teachers and opening opportunities for students that allow them to grasp portions of the problem as their own as they move through the problem-solving process.

Whose Problem?

The idea of real-world problems was grappled with in several of the classes. A problem to one set of students or to one teacher may not be a "real" problem to another set of students. The location of the problem seemed related to student interest in the problem. For example, if the problem is viewed as belonging to another country or being disconnected to students in their region, it may not seem as relevant or important to a group of students. Students taught us the importance of involving them in the beginning stages of identifying and selecting a real-world problem if we want them to consider the problem as "their" problem to solve. In Chapter 6, discussion about selection of problems will probe further into the topic of what makes a problem a problem.

Flexibility

Flexibility was critical when working with real-world problems and when encouraging students to become active in curriculum building. Most real-world problems do not have an apparent solution or an answer in the teacher's guide, so the path to finding a solution will not be in a straight line. Lessons deviated from original plans and moved in many directions at once as small groups of students explored and researched various topics connected to the problem. The teacher's responsibility shifted to facilitating discussions and helping students keep track of their findings and document research in a format that would allow students to share information with the larger group.

We found flexibility to be closely linked with several other important considerations as we moved through the real-world problem-solving units. Time allotted to the unit, both to the total unit and to individual lessons, required flexibility, most often in extending the time period to allow students to complete work to their satisfaction. Flexibility was also necessary when student interests diverged from their original plan or focus. Teachers found that when students could justify the focus they intended to pursue, generally the change was productive to the overall learning. We learned that when student interest and learning direct learning, the interchange is similar to the integrative grounding of the unit, with student interest and need also deriving access of knowledge from different disciplines.

Listening to Students

Several teachers noted that as they moved through the unit, they realized how critical it was to listen to their students and to pose essential questions that would help guide students to another step in their learning and research process. The teachers moved from providing direct information through instruction to listening to student discussions and helping students locate appropriate resources.

Dayle's students were proud of the surveys and research projects they completed on marketing or consumerism. Dayle listened to her students as they shared their research findings within the class and saw that their interest in sharing their findings could be moved to a wider audience. The posters and charts were displayed in the classroom for other students to observe. In addition, the students traveled to an elementary school and shared their findings with a class of second graders. This interchange was exciting to watch, as sixth, seventh, and eighth graders developed presentations that were meaningful to a younger audience. By listening to the enthusiasm displayed by her students, Dayle recognized and planned opportunities for presentations to a range of audiences. Her students gained experience in communicating their research, which reinforced the relevance of their work on the real-world problems.

When students in Susan's class were wondering about materials and resources used in shoes, she assisted them by looking through the telephone directory to locate a local shoe manufacturer, whom they asked to come and speak with the class. Students listened to the expert and asked questions to obtain information needed for their research. By listening to their discussions, Susan was able to note specific areas of interest and locate resources (in this case a "shoe manufacturing" expert) to assist in their learning. Students not only gained the information they were seeking but also learned how to access information in the future.

Expanding Integrative Teaching and Learning

Once students started working on real-world problem solving, their perspective on learning and engaging in activities in the classroom shifted to one of an active learner empowered to seek knowledge to solve an important problem. With this vision of learning in mind, teachers found themselves planning other lessons and units requiring integration of curriculum. The teachers noted that it became increasingly difficult to look at a subject area in isolation and that single subjects tended to seem artificial after experiencing integrative teaching and learning.

Interestingly, their students also noted the shift toward integration of subject areas and began to talk about subjects and topics in a problem-solving format. Kim's class worked with other teachers throughout the year, and following the "Salmon and Humans" unit, these students often turned topics presented by teachers into a problem that could then be researched. There were many conversations about problem solving, with their writing and later projects also reflecting their continued interest in integrative learning and problem solving.

At the end of the year, Susan asked her class to select three important areas that they had learned about during the entire school year and to rate her teaching in these three areas. The students selected reading, math, and shoes. Many of their written comments described the knowledge and skills they had gained through their work on the "Choosing Shoes" unit, with references to multiple disciplines and connections to their own lives.

Time

The teachers unanimously agreed that they had not scheduled enough time for the students to complete many of the activities and that more time was needed for the creation and presentation of the final product. Because this was the first integrative teaching unit these teachers had developed and taught, they were not experienced in estimating the time periods students needed to bring their information together and to work on the final projects. Students took great pride in their work and wanted to show the projects to the community, whether by a video presentation or some other kind of presentation to administrators, parents, or other students.

These teachers and students learned that it does takes more time for students to conduct research, report findings, and create meaning from their work in comparison to the amount of time it takes to read a worksheet or present a lecture on a topic. They also learned that students learned more and retained this knowledge when they were assessed at the end of the integrative unit. Because time is at a premium in the elementary classroom, some balance had to be found between time for the projects and time for other activities. Several teachers approached this dilemma by scheduling blocks of time 2 or 3 days per week over several months for the work on the real-world problem-solving unit, thereby allowing students to continue their work over a long period of time.

Planning an Integrative
Teaching and Learning Unit

How do you plan a unit that will be unfolding as the students develop interests and their own direction when pursuing a real-world problem? Teachers puzzled over this question and came to understand that planning conceptual and knowledge goals to create an overview of the unit was helpful but that specific plans would go through many changes as students progressed through problem solving. During implementation of the units, the teachers became more experienced listening to students and were able to shift the focus of the unit in the directions indicated by student questions, interest, and research.

There were many times when teachers documented the lesson plan following completion of the lesson, with this activity viewed as a sketch of a possible plan for a future unit or to help connect with future lessons within this real-world problem unit. During a discussion about planning, teachers agreed that they gave themselves permission to change their plans and felt this reflected constructivist thinking, with students shaping the learning and selecting activities to assist them in their problem solving. Nalani found that lesson plans were a guide and definitely not an absolute script. She noted there were many welcome surprises (teachable moments) that contributed to the unit's success and could not have been planned prior to the actual lesson.

Kim changed the last half of the real-world problem-solving unit when she became aware of student interest in writing. She had originally planned to have the students create a totem pole that would represent their learning in the "Native Americans" and the "Salmon and Humans" unit. Students began bringing newspaper articles about the salmon crisis to school on a regular basis. Several students talked about writing their own articles, drawing from their research about the coexistence of salmon and humans. Although several students chose to develop a totem pole, most of the class contributed articles to an edition of the *Northwest News*, which was published and distributed to parents, faculty, students, and agencies connected with the salmon issues. She learned that planning prior to the unit was important, but equally important was listening to her students and observing their work and interests and responding to these areas by assisting students in accessing resources needed to create a match between student interests and the goals of the real-world problem-solving unit. Again, flexibility, time, and listening to students were reported as important things they had learned and necessary for success in integrative teaching through real-world problem solving by the teachers.

Revising Teaching Based on
Student Interests and Needs

At the beginning of the units, several of the teachers had plans for involved, detailed lessons with many open-ended activities. They soon decided that they, as teachers, had planned too much, and that they would rather observe the students and follow their lead in setting the plans. One teacher found she could start with a specific focus, such as learning the external body parts of a salmon, and then provide several options for students to select from as they pursued their study of salmon. Several students worked together to draw salmon and name the body parts; other students drew a human figure (with gills and other fish parts) and labeled the body parts as salmon parts. Another group made a card game with the fish parts and played "Fish Parts" by drawing cards and naming the fish part on the card. She learned from earlier lessons that students needed some ideas presented as options so they could then either choose from these ideas or develop another way to learn the information.

Dayle commented that a difficult part of her teaching occurred at the beginning of the unit when she did not provide enough structure for this group of students. The students did not seem comfortable with choices or conducting research of their own and continually asked what information would be on the test and how would they be graded. In fact, the teacher felt the students did not take the assignments seriously because they were used to specific guidelines and assumed that the absence of direction from the teacher meant the work was not significant. After 3 or 4 days of muddling through their uncomfortable affect, she introduced some general guidelines yet still required student choices of topics and formats for completing assignments. As they moved through the unit, she was able to slowly remove some of the structure, placing more responsibility for choices into the students' hands. The students developed a rubric for assessing their final project and were pleased with the fairness and emphasis on quality of content and presentation that they had developed. We learned from these students that an integrative unit requires teaching students how to make their own learning choices and guiding their learning as they move through the real-world problem-solving process.

Cooperative Learning

Students were involved in different models of cooperative learning throughout each of the problem-solving units. In several situations, groups of students were responsible for conducting research needed by the entire class and reported a summary of their findings to the whole class. Other times students worked together when topics were similar or the research was conducted in a similar format. For instance, when several second graders were recording the different types of plants found in the wetlands area and drawing pictures of these specimens, they worked together to identify details such as leaf shape, stem size, or the color of plant. Discussing the plant features helped students note more of the plant features and more accurately describe the plant.

The teachers were pleased with the collaborative climate established with real-world problem solving and again saw the implementation of integrative teaching and learning through real-world problem solving as a foundation for student use of cooperative learning within a meaningful setting and a relevant purpose. Although the models of cooperative learning varied, the outcome was similar in each classroom. Students shared in the learning process and supported each other's work toward problem solving.

Students With Special Needs

The collaborative approach to problem solving enabled students with special needs to be contributing members of the class as students worked together. Each of the classes had several students identified as special needs students, but in this project, all students were actively involved in providing productive information toward the problem solving. As the problem solving led to activities that were guided by self-interest, students were able not only to fit into the classroom learning structure but also to choose activities that they could connect with, adding their expertise and information to the problem solving. In one class, a student with special needs created a clay model of a foot, which helped other students note the shape and needs of a foot when designing shoes. Her work was viewed as a contribution by the other students, making her a part of the learning community. The teachers were pleased with the numerous ways that students with special needs were able to be truly included throughout the problem solving.

Making Connections

One teacher stated, "I learned that jumping from topic to topic without making connections confuses students, even when we are on the same theme." Connections between topics, within the topic, and to real life are critical to creating true understanding of a topic or issue. We often assume that others will make the same connections, as if everyone will make the same leap to other information or topics that we make. Discussions about these connections and links within and across disciplines proved to be important in the learning and problem-solving process. Teachers learned that asking questions or challenging student responses or statements could help students link new information to knowledge they had worked with in the past.

Another important connection was one between the problem students were working with and current issues. Students in Dayle's class analyzed popular clothing styles and discussed how advertising affected choices students made in purchasing clothing. They also looked at advertisements from the 1960s and asked their parents about the clothing fads when they were middle school age.

Kim's students brought newspaper articles to school about salmon issues and also taped television news segments related to Native American fishing rights and the decreasing salmon population. Although the final projects for the "Salmon and Humans" unit were completed in early May, students continued bringing in articles and discussing the salmon issues until the end of the school year. These students had made a connection between the problem they had studied and the current solutions presented by different agencies and groups. Through experience and by listening to our students, we learned the importance of helping students make connections in their work, not only between disciplines (e.g., impact on natural resources used in shoe production required students to use mathematics, social studies, and science) but also between their real-world problem and related current issues.

Summary

Perhaps one of the most vivid lessons we learned with the development and implementation of the integrative teaching and learning units was summarized by one of the students, Jason: "You won't believe it! Even fifth graders can learn to make real shoes. My company has pulled up from making two shoes in 40 minutes to making 14 shoes in 100 minutes." These students commented over and over again that they were involved in learning "real things," whether the real thing was salmon ("The salmon population is dwindling. We should make it a law to require people to put screens over pipes that go to irrigation systems so fish would not get sucked into the irrigation pipes."—Joseph, fifth grade), making wise purchases ("Sometimes the thing we want to buy was made from nature and hurts our environment. We can find out about the materials used in the things we buy and make decisions with this information."—Jeremy, fifth grade), deciphering commercials ("The surveying project allowed more creativity than is usually allowed in math. It's good you had us do projects instead of endless worksheets."—Colin, seventh grade), or deciding what to do with the front yard of a school ("Wetlands are getting smaller. Did you know wetlands help by making homes for animals?"—Amir, second grade). *Real* took on a life of its own, enabling students to become involved in meaningful, important issues. This approach to teaching and learning does require more time and energy on the teacher's part when compared to following a teacher's guide in a textbook. But our teachers tell us that the increased time and energy are worthwhile. They find themselves enjoying learning with their students, see more results in learning and motivation to learn, and find an increase in positive energy flowing throughout the classroom when students are engaged in problem solving.

The students taught us that if we listen to them and watch their learning progress as they solve real-world problems, we come to understand the importance of bringing real-world experiences and integrative learning into the classroom. Student learning and involvement revealed the depth and interest in learning that can occur when students are engaged in integrative teaching and learning through solving real-world problems. Our students were immersed in real learning as they discovered the importance of researching important issues and presenting their findings to their community.

6

Looking Ahead

SUGGESTIONS FOR IMPLEMENTATION

Involve students from the very beginning in the planning and exploration of the problem. The strongest learning occurred when students were involved in researching and presenting information about topics of interest to them.

—Dayle Spitzer, middle school math teacher

Introducing Integrative Teaching and Learning and Problem Solving

Prior to developing a problem-solving unit with students, teachers might want to look at their current teaching and learning approach and note similarities and differences between current practice and a problem-solving approach. Dayle found her students (sixth, seventh, and eighth graders) unfamiliar with the experience of making choices for the direction of their learning. If she were to work with students at this age level again, and with a group of students who seemed to have had minimal experience with self-directed learning, she would start with small components of the problem-solving approach and build on these experiences prior to starting the entire problem-solving unit.

For example, if students are accustomed to assignments following a format, with each student completing an identical assignment, a teacher might start providing options for assignments, with students choosing their assignment from the list of options. As students become comfortable with choosing from a teacher-generated list, the next step might be to present these options plus the additional option of any student presenting an alternative assignment option. Students would gain experience in generating options or formats for assignments of interest to themselves, leading to more student-directed learning and increased engagement throughout the learning process.

Once students are successful in selecting and completing different types of assignments, the teacher might then ask them to think of criteria for assessing their work. This discussion could include developing rubrics or criteria-based scores for assignments. Listening to them and recording their ideas on charts helps students realize the teacher is recognizing their ideas and input into their learning. Students also gain a clear idea of the expectations for the assignment and learning and for the guidelines or criteria established to assess the learning.

Each group of students differs in its experiences with open-ended units and/or student-directed learning. Through observations and interactions with students, the teacher will be able to judge the students' level of experience and background in student-directed projects and plan a continuum of activities based on prior experience and comfort level in assuming responsibility for their learning. By incorporating into the classroom the suggestions outlined in this section, students are building toward the integrative teaching and learning approach in which they will be involved when working with real-world problem solving.

What Makes a Problem a Problem?

All four teachers were adamant about wishing that they had spent more time with their students in identifying and selecting the real-world problem prior to the beginning of the unit. Students who felt the problem was truly their problem were more invested in the learning process and interpreted problem solving as an exciting and challenging activity. The teachers recommend taking time prior to beginning the unit to talk about problems, explore problem solving, and help students decide if the topic is a real-world problem and what makes a problem a real-world problem. This activity is essential to introducing real-world problem solving in the format of an integrative teaching and learning unit, as students begin to create a web of concepts, knowledge, and skills needed from multiple disciplines to address their problem and possible solutions to their problem.

Suggestions for deciding if a topic might be viewed as a problem include examining the topic with the students to note if there are any issues or parts of the topic that are controversial to the students or community members, if students disagree about the topic or outcomes of the topic, or if there are notably apparent solutions to the problem. Another helpful approach to determining if this is a problem of interest is to compare the potential problem to typical problems encountered by students, their families, and community members. A major difference between teaching a topic and teaching around problem solving is found in the notion of presenting predetermined information or a static curriculum versus teaching and learning that revolve around an emergent curriculum related to the problem and problem-solving process. Although several classes may select to work on similar problems, their research and problem-solving process will differ according to interests and directions students bring to and develop during problem solving. Developing and applying criteria constructed by the students when deciding what makes a problem worth studying is the next step in selecting a real-world problem for a unit of study.

Susan recommends looking at the curriculum outline for the grade level you are teaching and identifying key areas of interest that might also be reflected in a real-world problem. She feels that the link between the required curriculum and the content of the real-world problem would provide the luxury of more time available for the real-world problem-solving unit, creating a natural fit between school district curriculum requirements and the integrative unit.

The initial work in identifying and selecting the real-world problem pays off in great dividends when students become invested in solving the problem and view it as meaningful and important. Spending time exploring the problem prior to deciding if this is the real-world problem students wish to work on allows the students to capture the problem and shape the problem into an area of interest to them.

Developing a Problem Statement
or Unit Overview

Once a problem has been selected, creating a problem statement that is clearly understood by all learners is essential. Two suggestions in forming the problem statement are to examine possible statements for specificity (allows students enough focus to work through a long-term problem-solving process) and for relevance to students' life experiences. We found the most meaningful problem situations were those that students connected with and found solutions in which they could be involved. A real-world problem that is perceived to be important by the students empowers them to play a role in our world and teaches them that their ideas and work have credibility.

Sharing the problem statement with parents, colleagues, community members, and experts involved in the problem provides feedback about the problem and begins to build a resource base for problem solving. The teachers suggest involving other points of view as much as possible, because this will open up investigations and solutions.

Moving from exploring topics to selecting a problem area to creating a problem statement is an important part of the problem-solving process. The definition process assists in helping students gain ownership of the problem and brings clarity and focus to the unit.

Planning the Integrative Unit

Planning the unit provides a foundation and structure and helps establish an overview of possible directions the unit may take. In addition, a general overview assists in identifying potential resources for the unit. Providing and locating resources are essential to the problem-solving process, and often, it will take time to contact experts, write letters, wait for responses to written or phone inquiries, or locate materials needed for research. Students need to be able to access as many resources as possible and to approach the problem from multiple disciplines and angles. For this to happen, numerous resources are needed.

Unit Goals

After a problem statement and unit overview have been developed, the next step is to plan general goals and objectives for the unit. Each teacher created general goals for the unit related to the problem statement. The unit goals provide direction and link the problem to curricular areas. In developing a goal, the teachers reviewed the student input on problem selection, assessing specific areas of interest and accommodating this interest in the development of goal statements.

The unit goals for Kim's unit (see case study in Chapter 3) state, "Students explore the interrelationship between salmon and humans and the historical and current importance of this interdependency." The goal is broad enough to allow different students to select areas or pieces of the unit that they are most interested in, yet the goal provides enough focus to begin planning activities and objectives and locating resources.

Lesson Plans and Activities

Following development of a goal for the unit, teachers and students then discussed the goal in terms of problem-solving steps or activities that might lead to possible solutions. A list of activities was created, which then guided lesson plans and activities. Often the list of activities and the lesson plans were a "brainstorm" and not necessarily presented in a sequential order. Through class discussions of activities or projects that might lead to problem solving, students listened to each other's thinking and came up with new ideas based on the active interchange.

Nalani recommends looking at lesson plans as a guide, but not as an absolute script. We want students to make their own meaning of their learning, integrate their prior knowledge with their current research, and test possible solutions to the problems. Many times, real-world problems do not have an answer or have an answer that is not apparent, so students must tackle the unknown through their own lens on learning. Thinking of preplanning as a guide but not an absolute allows many surprises (teachable moments) to occur that might have been thwarted if the teacher followed a predetermined plan that led to a specific end.

Each of the teachers found that flexibility throughout the unit encouraged students to take more responsibility for the direction of the learning and for guiding the problem-solving process. Each teacher came to recognize the role that flexibility played in student learning through the experience of integrative teaching and learning. Kim found her students so interested in the temperature of the aquarium and the relation between water temperature and hatching date of the salmon that she altered her role in order to share the responsibility for aquarium monitoring. Students wanted authentic ownership and responsibility in their learning process.

Most of the lesson plans presented in Chapter 3 were modified during the teaching of the unit and rewritten to reflect the actual lesson that took place. The teachers reminded each other that the written units could be shared with each other or used with a new class, but only if the students were indeed interested in the problem. The teachers recognized that each group of students would create its own direction for the unit, even if the problem statement or unit overview were similar to the existing units. Interestingly though, the teachers did not feel they wasted time by creating plans that were altered or in some cases not even used. The planning process helped them think through alternative activities that students might be interested in and helped explore additional avenues for approaching the problem.

Planning the unit also provided a way for the teachers to look at different curriculum areas and make connections between the disciplines. For example, when Susan's class was studying about shoes, she brought in books about Jan Matzeliger, who invented the shoe-lasting machine. Several students became interested in his work and the struggles he went through in his life. These students chose to develop a timeline for Matzeliger's life and looked at other events occurring during this time period. They also created a project that illustrated the economic, social, and political climate during the early 1900s, when his work was ongoing. Clearly these students were exploring social studies as a part of the unit.

Nalani wanted to ensure that her students were using math skills and concepts they had learned earlier in the year, so she developed several lessons that required measuring and the use of fractions. The connection between the math work and the importance of obtaining accurate information leading to valid research was obvious to the students. Not only were they working on solving a real problem, but their prior learning was being used in a "real" application.

With the "Salmon and Humans" unit, Kim found her fifth graders making numerous connections between disciplines. Study of Native Americans is a curriculum requirement for her grade level, and the connection between the "Salmon and Humans" unit and Native Americans was a natural occurrence. She found it easy to plan lessons that connected and used mathematics (measuring temperature), social studies (history of the region), communication (writing, reading, and oral presentations), science (cycle of salmon development), and art (drawings and creations of salmon representations in Native American style).

Looking at the activities and plans as a guide or outline for the integrative unit enabled the teachers to ensure that connections between disciplines, prior knowledge, and student interests were present. Teachers were also able to incorporate skills, knowledge, and information critical to problem solving in earlier lessons, which then created a knowledge base for students as they selected their own interests to pursue within problem solving. The planning period was also viewed as an interactive resource-gathering period. Students, parents, other teachers, and staff at the school were important resources during the planning period.

Ensuring That Student Interests Guide the Unit

Once plans are outlined around the unit goal and activities, the teachers felt that students and their individual or collective interests should create the paths leading to a solution for the real-world problem. The starting place would be the unit goal, with the activities and research leading to the problem solution.

Susan reinforced the idea that trying to fit every related topic to the problem creates overload. She emphasized the need to focus on the problem, not a topic, and allow the problem-solving process to guide the curriculum. There will not be an equal balance or distribution of each discipline within an integrative teaching and learning unit. Attempting to push each discipline into the unit creates an uncomfortable fit and moves the unit away from the intent of allowing the problem-solving process to unfold as students gain new knowledge, apply findings, and share their research.

Recording and reviewing student input is important in looking at original thoughts and reviewing the problem-solving process as more is learned. Revisions to original plans or new areas to research may need to be explored throughout the process. Nalani stressed the importance of listening to her students and remaining flexible in changing plans as student focus shifted. This does not mean switching the focus anytime someone has a new idea, but flexibility is important to allowing student learning and interest shape the next steps. As the teachers and students experienced the integrative teaching and learning, they became more comfortable with changing directions or adding to or deleting from prior directions. The teachers were clear about the importance of giving up some of their control over the problem-solving process to help students become empowered in their own sense making of their learning.

Time

Each teacher found she wished for more time to increase the depth of the problem-solving process. The integrative teaching and learning unit was very different from other teaching experiences in this sense. Students quickly became engrossed in their research and found limited time periods frustrating when they needed time to make connections between their findings and the direction they were heading in problem solving. Nalani found it important to hold continual "update" sessions, where students shared their current findings and posed questions for the class. Their work-in-progress was posted on charts around the room, capturing a visual representation of the work and process the students were conducting.

The fifth graders in Kim's class selected the problem-solving approach to many different units and activities for the remainder of the school year. Once they had experienced the real-world problem experience and integrative learning, they would look at new units through this experience and try to shape the unit into the problem-solving format. The teachers who worked with these students encouraged them to continue with their problem-solving approach, which resulted in teachers working together to plan for shared time blocks and related activities. There was a demand for more time for collaborative teacher planning and for student research in their problem solving. The integrative teaching and learning led to interesting connections between disciplines, most notably with the science, social studies, fine arts, and language arts curricular areas. The science specialist worked with Kim and her students throughout the school year to build future units based on the foundation established in the salmon unit. For example, the science specialist presented other topics in light of the students' understanding of cycles, which was clearly represented in the life cycle of a salmon. Integrative teaching and planning does demand time for planning and time to listen to students and their interests to be successful in truly looking at teaching and learning from a constructivist perspective and in an integrative format.

Dayle noted the high level of interest her students expressed in conducting their own survey and research project and wanted to find an avenue that would enable the students to share their learning with others. Kim's students wanted to create a newspaper and write articles about their research findings related to salmon and humans. Susan's students were eager to both show off the baby shoes they had constructed and give them to mothers and babies. The second graders wanted to take more people out to their wetlands area and tell them about the importance of wetlands and the function this particular wetland served in their community. Each of these activities is meaningful and relevant and requires the limited commodity of time. Looking back at the units, the teachers commented on the importance of attending to the wishes of the students to share their learning. Students were immersed in real-world problems, and these problems do affect the community. Thus students were engaged in exploring solutions and wanted to share their research and solutions with more groups. The teachers strongly suggest building in enough time at the end of the project so students can present and share their solutions with several audiences.

Culminating Event or Final Project

The final project or major production from the integrative teaching and learning unit serves the purpose of providing a format for students to share their knowledge and to propose possible solutions for a real-world problem. The final project was an opportunity for students (individually or in small groups) to pursue and research their specific interests as connected to problem solving. After all, working through a real-world problem and reaching a real solution deserve presentation to a real audience.

Photo 6.1. Dayle's Sixth-, Seventh-, and Eighth-Grade Students
Traveled to Visit Second Graders and Present Their Survey Findings

Final projects were seen as a highlight of the integrative teaching
and learning unit, both from the students' and the teachers' perspective.
Dayle noted that her favorite part of the unit was the final project, during
which students presented their surveys and research findings to each
other and later to a class of second graders. She found that the project
allowed for individual student interest, active involvement, and
student choice. The project was also a summation of the unit and
students had an opportunity to share and view how other students
conducted their surveys and presented research findings.

Several examples of final projects include a forum or town hall
type of meeting, a video production and presentation, an assembly
at the school, an evening presentation for the neighborhood, a network conference over computer or television, a meeting at a business
or agency connected to the real-world problem, publications, or a
demonstration or presentation at a community event. The teachers
found that students wanted to share their work with parents, community members, and experts in fields related to the real-world
problem. With several classes, the students wanted to share their
findings with younger students, so that these students might become

better educated about the real-world problem and thus become part of the solution.

During the preparation for the final project, teachers were aware of the students' sense of ownership of the problem and a solution to the problem. Developing a project that stayed within the confines of a classroom minimized the work the students had completed and seemed to contradict the intent of real-world problem solving. Students wanted an audience and they also wanted others to understand the importance of the real-world problem and the need for a solution to the problem.

For instance, Nalani's second graders became gatekeepers to the wetlands area in their front yard. Several parents and community members had suggested paving the area or landscaping the wetland, because it looked "unsightly." The second graders made their views and knowledge known to the community, by developing and presenting a video explaining the impact of this small wetland within the community. Ending the project by merely drawing a picture or writing a story to be graded was not the intent of these students. They wanted community support for maintaining "their" wetlands area. Obviously, the integrative teaching and learning unit moved far beyond the classroom walls and a report card. This was a real problem and the second graders developed and presented a real solution to a real audience.

Integrative Learning and Final Projects

As students moved toward putting their findings and potential solutions into a final project format, multiple disciplines were continually accessed in the design and implementation of the final project. Students worked with mathematics in interpreting and reporting statistics, percentages, fractions, measurements, temperatures, and other information. Communication skills were needed in writing letters and reports, giving oral reports or presentations, listening to and answering questions at forums or meetings, and communicating with the audience. Students dabbled in fine arts when drawing posters or pictures of their findings, composing music for their work, or selecting music for their video presentation. In each of the units, the sciences provided a format for experimenting, investigating, and hypothesizing and testing the presumptions, along with the concepts and knowledge accessed in each unit. Social studies was important

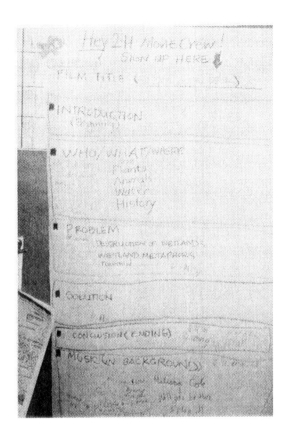

Photo 6.2. The Movie Crew (Nalani's Second Graders) Sign-Up Sheet for Responsibilities in the Production of the Wetland Video

in each unit; for example, Susan's students studied the history of shoes and the use of resources in shoe production. The flow between and among the disciplines was natural and provided for rich, meaningful research and insights throughout the real-world problem-solving process.

Documenting the Final Event

Each teacher found that the final project or event was a major highlight of the school year. They unanimously recommend recording or documenting the event, whether through videotaping, photographs, or audio recordings. By documenting the event, students have the opportunity to revisit their work and discuss the important learnings and suggestions that have come from their problem solving.

Nalani was able to develop a video of the "Our Front Yard" unit, documenting student activities and thoughts about the unit from the beginning lesson to the final project. Through grant funding, she was able to provide a copy of the videotape for each student. The other teachers kept cameras in the class and developed an album of the problem-solving unit. Two of the teachers had double prints developed and made packets of photographs for the students. The families appreciated the photographs and videos and felt included in their children's learning.

Final Thoughts and Recommendations
From the Teachers and Students

Dayle recommends trying out a variety of teaching ideas and approaches. She reminds others not to expect 100% success with the project, because this is a learning experience for teachers as well as students. But she also found the experience to be fun for her and the students and learned that sharing her insights and observations and working together with the students created a collaborative atmosphere that allowed students to gain ownership of their learning.

Susan found that the integrative teaching and learning experience influenced her thinking about future units and the possibilities of curriculum integration and real-world units. She believes she was heavily influenced because this type of unit appealed to each student in some way. She found that "real-world problems that replicate and make as real as possible the world we share seem to be a more honest way of teaching our students to be successful in the future."

Recommendations from Kim include looking at real-world problem solving as a connection between the school and life outside the school. She learned the importance of allowing the unfolding of a problem through student exploration and research and found it resulted in the students taking responsibility for their own learning as they make connections to their daily lives.

The second graders found that they were able to impact their community. Nalani posed the question of deciding what to do with the front yard of the school and developed lessons and activities that allowed the students to research possibilities, learn about wetlands and the environment, and reach decisions about an important community concern through their research. These students were empowered through real-world problem solving and their involvement in integrative teaching and learning. Nalani recommends listening carefully to the students' concerns and questions that they raise about the real-world problem and their research. She also suggests scheduling large blocks of time for work on the real-world problem and for students to bring together their findings and explore emergent questions and issues. Both of these recommendations lead to a student-centered learning environment and enable students to delve into an important subject area of high interest and relevance.

Implementing any new instructional or curricular program involves change and risks. Our experiences with real-world problem solving and integrative teaching and learning taught us a new way of thinking about teaching and learning. We view ourselves as cocurriculum partners with our students. The depth of student involvement in problem solving motivates us to encourage other educators to consider bringing the excitement of relevant and meaningful learning through real-world problem solving to their students.

7

Making Integrative Teaching and Learning Happen

To consider large purposes is also to fashion a more integrated curriculum, one that stresses continuities, not divisions, between disciplines, in which topics are revisited often, and grade levels and the clock do not "limit" what students learn, where students have the time needed to do work that they can honor, that helps them build a culture of high standards and quality.

—Vito Perrone (1991, p. 165)

Preparing Students for the Future

Students of today are entering a world that demands continuous learning. Looking into the late 1990s and beyond finds tremendous changes in the technology used in the workplace and in the home. Computers and the information highway will play major roles in bringing us the current news and information as events or activities occur.

Learning how to learn and how to access essential and timely information or data will be a primary goal of education. Information and knowledge will be transmitted on networks or on-line, with schools tapping into the network systems. As we move through the information explosion, memorizing increasing amounts of knowledge will become impossible, and the emphasis in learning will shift from reading textbooks and taking tests on textbook material to learning how to access, process, and synthesize information. These demands and shifts will require a different curriculum and teaching and learning format in the classroom.

The integrative teaching and learning model encourages students to tap into current information, examine past experiences related to the problem they are working with, and pull their findings together to create useful solutions or proposals. The learning is seamless, with multiple disciplines accessed as needed in the acquisition of knowledge for the purpose of problem solving. Students engage in learning that is relevant and meaningful, because they acquire knowledge and skills necessary to access and analyze information and present solutions to real-world problems.

Reform in Education and Real-World Problem Solving

Reform in education is rampant at the national, state, and local levels. Ideas and mandates spring up at a surprising rate, with little time for educators to become reeducated or reflect on the reform mandates before changes are made. Currently, educators are thrust into a world of change in their workplace. Change is here and it is crucial to understand the ideas behind reform measures and the results of restructuring efforts.

One of the major changes in education is found in the movement toward mastery of learning, including demonstration or application of mastery of skills, knowledge, and understanding of curriculum. At the same time we are moving away from obtaining a traditional credit or grade by meeting "seat-time" requirements for specified classes. Real-world problem solving requires students to use their skills and knowledge to create an understanding of the problems along with solutions to these problems. Students also demonstrate their learning gains through presentations and products created throughout the real-world problem solving process. Integrative teaching and learning through real-world problem solving provides a rich learning environment that is in alignment with educational restructuring, with an emphasis on relevant learning and demonstration of mastery of this learning a major component of both restructuring and real-world problem solving.

Other reform measures addressed in real-world problem solving are the emphasis on activities selected by students and on collaborative work. Both of these measures promote student involvement in their learning and allow students to work together to accomplish important tasks. Employers are communicating to the public and to educators that there exists a critical need to hire graduates with the ability to not only work with others but also to learn new skills and knowledge in the ever-changing workplace.

Many of the students in school today will be entering jobs that have yet to be developed. Educators must help students learn how to learn and gain the tools needed to continue learning as the workplace and the world change throughout their lives. Involvement in real-world problem solving teaches students how to find information, locate and contact resources and experts, and bring their new knowledge together and share it with peers to create solutions to critical problems. These skills and experiences gained in problem solving are the same skills and abilities sought by employers.

Changes in Schooling

Creating and implementing new curricular and instructional models require a strong commitment from teachers, administrators, parents, and students. Teachers who are clear about their vision of teaching and learning and can communicate an understanding of best practices of educating children are in a position to communicate their knowledge to other educators. Integrative teaching and learning changes the classroom as we know it now. New expectations for teaching and learning will emerge as students experience integrative teaching and learning.

One shift that occurs as integrative teaching and learning is embraced in a school is the shift from teaching specific curriculum in a fragmented format to an emphasis on the students as active learners, with the teacher guiding their learning throughout a problem-solving process and using multiple disciplines as needed. James Moffett (1992b) reminds us that

> Finally, the master argument for curricular integration is
> simply that life is not divided into subjects. This argument
> may be grounded in either personal or social reality. That
> is, academic departments fit neither the way individuals
> build their personal knowledge structures nor the way so-
> cietal problems arise to which knowledge may be applied.
> (p. 83)

He clearly states the importance of acknowledging how people learn
and how people use their knowledge in life. The real-world problem-
solving process promotes the active integrative sense of learning
through student-directed work on issues of concern to both the
students and the larger community. Real-world problem solving is
real work and follows the same process that individuals and groups
use in everyday life.

Gaining Support

Change is never easy and may move slower (or faster) than some
educators prefer. In some schools, teams of teachers or individual
teachers may decide to implement real-world problem solving in
their classrooms. Following their teaching and learning experiences
and sharing of these experiences with colleagues, other teachers tend
to become interested in the real-world problem-solving process. It is
hard to miss the enthusiasm generated about school and learning by
students and teachers working on problem solving. Through actual
implementation of a real-world problem-solving unit, teachers and
students gain a greater understanding of and appreciation for a
learning experience focused on student interests, relevant topics, and
actual use of knowledge from many disciplines.

For teachers to successfully implement integrative curriculum,
support from others, most notably administrators, colleagues, and
the community, is important (Braunger & Hart-Landsberg, 1994).
Moving from separate curriculum segments to an integrative learning experience requires a shift from the traditional classroom setting.
Students and teachers will be accessing information from the community and beyond the community as they work through real-world
problem solving. Textbooks and seat work assignments will not be
the norm. Students will be making telephone calls, writing letters,

inviting speakers to the classroom, and visiting experts in the field. Teachers and their students become advocates of problem solving as they share the purpose and intent of real-world problem solving with other students, colleagues, administrators, and the larger community to gain their support and assistance as students progress through the problem solving.

The four teachers who presented their real-world problem units in this book found support through frequent discussions and sharing of ideas and resources with their colleagues, who were also involved in developing and teaching real-world problem-solving units. The teachers worked in different schools yet were able to come together to support one another in the integrative teaching and learning experience. They repeatedly stressed the value of meeting with colleagues as they moved through their own teaching and learning experiences.

As these positive and relevant learning experiences are shared with the larger community within the school and outside of school, expectations for learning begin reinforcing the change cycle as more educators, parents, students, and community members realize the value and success of integrative teaching and learning through real-world problem solving.

Taking It From Here: Your Turn

The work shared by the four teachers in this book is presented as a beginning point for other educators interested in implementing integrative teaching and learning through real-world problem solving. Real-world problem solving provides a solid foundation and context for learning that allows students to learn from many disciplines as they access and apply knowledge in a meaningful format. The ideas from Nalani, Susan, Kim, and Dayle, along with input from their students and the larger community, add to a newly created knowledge base on integrative teaching and learning. Looking into these four classrooms provides a glimpse of meaningful learning, occurring within the context of student-centered learning through problem solving.

A classroom that embraces problem solving provides numerous opportunities for critical thinking, student-centered learning, and a relevant, coherent curriculum. It is our hope that presenting a frame-work of integrative learning and teaching and a rationale for real-world problem solving and sharing these experiences along with the teachers' and students' reflections on real-world problem solving, will motivate other teachers to create their own integrative teaching and learning environments, based on their students' interests and community needs.

References

Alexander, W., & McEwin, C. K. (1989). *Schools in the middle: Status and programs.* Columbus, OH: National Middle School Association.

American Association for the Advancement of Science (AAAS). (1989). *Science for all Americans: Project 2061.* Washington, DC: Author.

Beane, J. A. (1992). *Integrated curriculum in the middle school. ERIC digest.* Washington, DC: Office of Educational Research and Improvement.

Beane, J. A. (1993). Problems and possibilities for an integrative curriculum. *Middle School Journal, 25*(1), 18-23.

Benjamin, S. (1989). An ideascape for education: What futurists recommend. *Educational Leadership, 47*(1), 8-16.

Braunger, J., & Hart-Landsberg, S. (1994). *Crossing boundaries: Explorations in integrative curriculum.* Portland, OR: Northwest Regional Educational Laboratory.

Brooks, J. G., & Brooks, M. G. (1993). *In search of understanding: The case for constructivist classrooms.* Alexandria, VA: Association for Supervision and Curriculum Development.

Carnegie Council. (1989). *Turning points: Preparing American youth for the 21st century.* Washington, DC: Carnegie Council on Adolescent Development.

Dewey, J. (1938). *Experience and education.* New York: Macmillan.

Fogarty, R. (1991). *The mindful school: How to integrate the curricula.* Palatine, IL: IRI/Skylight.

Freiberg, H. J., & Driscoll, A. (1992). *Universal teaching strategies.* Needham Heights, MA: Allyn & Bacon.

Fulwiler, T. (1987). *Teaching with writing.* Portsmouth, NH: Boynton/Cook.

Gardner, H. (1993). *Multiple intelligences: The theory in practice.* New York: Basic Books.

Gardner, H., & Boix-Mansilla, V. (1994). Teaching for understanding—Within and across the disciplines. *Educational Leadership, 51*(5), 14-18.

Gutek, G. L. (1991). *An historical introduction to American education.* Prospect Heights, IL: Waveland.

Henning-Stout, M. (1994). *Responsive assessment: A new way of thinking about learning.* San Francisco: Jossey-Bass.

Homans, G. C. (1965). Group factors in worker productivity. In H. Proshansky & L. Seidenberg (Eds.), *Basic studies in social psychology* (pp. 592-604). New York: Henry Holt.

Joyce, B. R., Weil, M., with Showers, B. (1992). *Models of teaching.* Needham Heights, MA: Allyn & Bacon.

Meyer, C. A. (1992). What's the difference between "authentic" and "performance" assessment? *Educational Leadership, 49*(8), 39-40.

Moffett, J. (1992a). *Active voice: A writing program across the curriculum* (2nd ed.). Portsmouth, NH: Heinemann.

Moffett, J. (1992b). *Harmonic learning: Keynoting school reform.* Portsmouth, NH: Heinemann.

National Commission on Excellence in Education. (1983). *A nation at risk: The imperative for educational reform.* Washington DC: Author.

National Council of Teachers of Mathematics (NCTM). (1989). *Curriculum and evaluation standards for school mathematics.* Reston, VA: Author.

Noddings, N. (1990). Constructivism in mathematics education [Monograph]. *Journal for Research in Mathematics Education, 4,* 7-18.

Pace, G. E. (1992). *Making decisions about grouping in language arts.* Literacy Improvement Series for Elementary Educators, Literacy, Language and Communication Program. Portland, OR: Northwest Regional Educational Laboratory.

Perkins, D. N. (1992). *Smart schools: From training memories to educating minds.* New York: Macmillan.

Perkins, D. N., & Blythe, T. (1994). Putting understanding up front. *Educational Leadership, 51*(5), 4-7.

Perrone, V. (1991). Toward more powerful assessment. In V. Perrone (Ed.), *Expanding student assessment* (pp. 164-166). Alexandria, VA: Association for Supervision and Curriculum Development.

Perrone, V. (1994). How to engage students in learning. *Educational Leadership, 51*(5), 11-13.

Roth, W. M. (1993). Problem-centered learning for the integration of mathematics and science in a constructivist laboratory: A case study. *School Science and Mathematics, 93*(3), 113-122.

Routman, R. (1991). *Invitations: Changing as teachers and learners K-12.* Portsmouth, NH: Heinemann.

Rudner, L. M., & Boston, C. (1994). Performance assessment. *ERIC Review, 3*(1), 2-12.

Rutherford, F. J., & Ahlgren, A. (1990). *Science for all Americans.* New York: Oxford University Press.

Shavelson, R., & Baxter, G. (1992). What we've learned about assessing hands-on science. *Educational Leadership, 49*(8), 20-25.

Shoemaker, B. (1989). *Integrative education: A curriculum for the twenty-first century.* Eugene, OR: Oregon School Study Council.

Shuman, R. (1984). English in the curriculum: Education, society, and the second millennium. *NASSP Bulletin, 68*(474), 95-103.

Siegel, J., & Shaughnessy, M. (1994). Educating for understanding: An interview with Howard Gardner. *Phi Delta Kappan, 75*(7), 563-566.

Sizer, T. (1986). Rebuilding: First steps by the Coalition of Essential Schools. *Phi Delta Kappan, 68*(1), 38-42.

Stiggins, R. J. (1991). Assessment literacy. *Phi Delta Kappan, 72*(7), 534-539.

Suchman, J. R. (1962). *The elementary school training program in scientific inquiry* (U.S. Office of Education, Project Title VII, Project 216). Urbana: University of Illinois.

Sunstein, B. S. (1992). Introduction. In D. H. Graves & B. S. Sunstein (Eds.), *Portfolio portraits* (pp. xi-xvii). Portsmouth, NH: Heinemann.

Tiner, R. W. (1984). *Wetlands of the United States: Current status and recent trends.* Washington, DC: U.S. Fish and Wildlife Services.

Toffler, A. (1981). Education and the future. *Social Education, 45*(6), 422-426.

Valentine, J. W., Clark, D. C., Irvin, J. L., Keefe, J. W., & Melton, G. (1993). *Leadership in middle level education: Vol. 1. A national survey of middle level leaders and schools.* Reston, VA: National Association of Secondary School Principles.

von Glaserfeld, E. (1987). Learning as a constructivist activity. In C. Janvier (Ed.), *Problems of representation in the teaching and learning of mathematics* (pp. 3-17). Hillsdale, NJ: Lawrence Erlbaum.

Voss, M. (1992). Porfolios in first grade: A teacher's discoveries. In D. H. Graves & B. S. Sunstein (Eds.), *Portfolio portraits* (pp. 17-33). Portsmouth, NH: Heinemann.

Watson, D. (1989). Defining and describing whole language. *Elementary School Journal, 90*(2), 129-141.

Wiggins, G. (1992). Creating tests worth taking. *Educational Leadership, 49*(8), 26-33.

Author Index

Subject Index

CORWIN
PRESS

Printed in the United States
21126LVS00008B/178